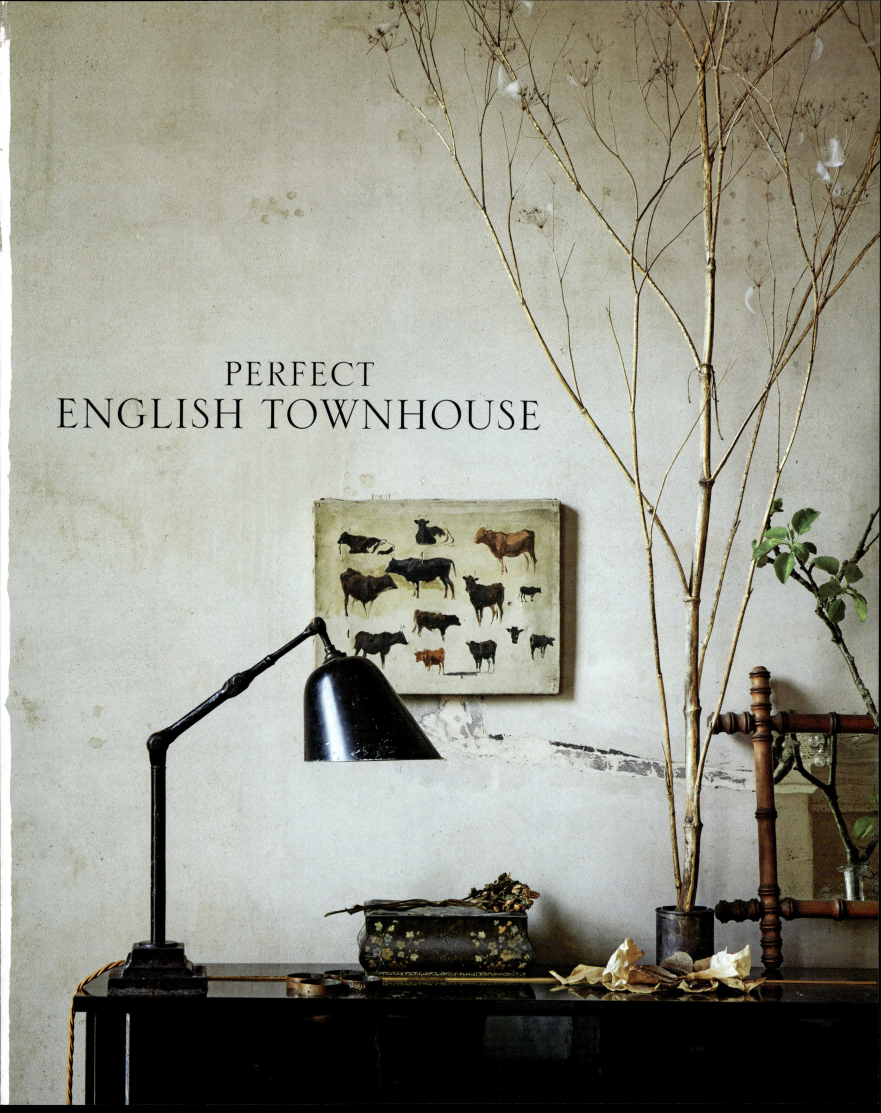

PERFECT
ENGLISH TOWNHOUSE

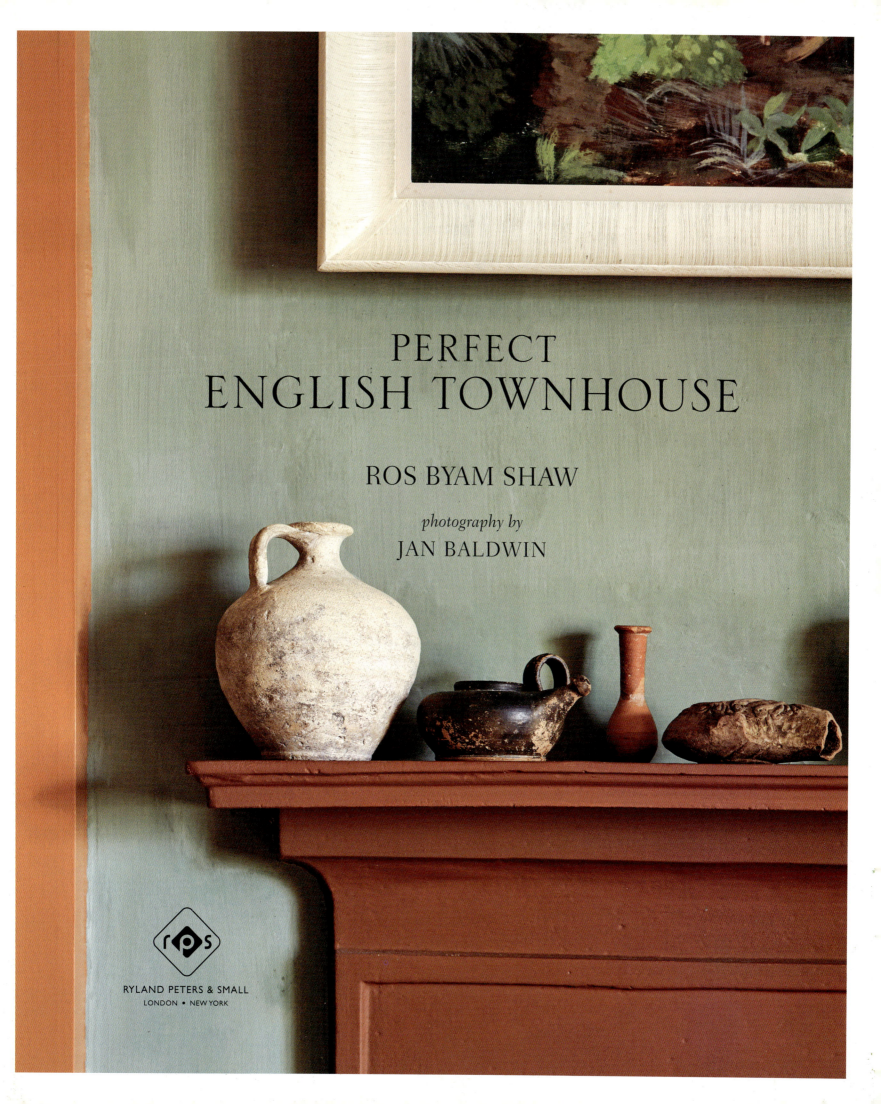

PERFECT
ENGLISH TOWNHOUSE

ROS BYAM SHAW

photography by
JAN BALDWIN

RYLAND PETERS & SMALL
LONDON • NEW YORK

FOR GEORGE

Senior designer Toni Kay
Senior commissioning editor Annabel Morgan
Location research Jess Walton
Production manager Gordana Simakovic
Art director Leslie Harrington
Editorial director Julia Charles
Publisher Cindy Richards

First published in 2018 by
Ryland Peters & Small
20–21 Jockey's Fields,
London WC1R 4BW
and
341 East 116th Street
New York, NY 10029

www.rylandpeters.com

Text copyright © Ros Byam Shaw
2018
Design and photographs copyright
© Ryland Peters & Small 2018

10 9 8 7 6 5 4

ISBN 978-1-84975-924-3

A CIP record for this book is available
from the British Library.

Library of Congress CIP data has been
applied for.

Printed and bound in China

MIX
Paper from
responsible sources
FSC® C106563
www.fsc.org

CONTENTS

INTRODUCTION

If there is one thing above all else that characterizes the English townhouse, it is stairs. Where land is valuable and space limited, you build up or you dig down. The skyscrapers that increasingly dominate and define the urban skyline are one symptom, and loft conversions their townhouse shadow. The 'mole' builders who carve out swimming pools, steam rooms, gyms, party rooms for teenagers, and, inevitably, bedrooms for the live-in help beneath the stucco facades of London's Kensington and Mayfair are another.

Subterranean gyms and skyscrapers are a relatively modern phenomenon, but the principle of vertical growth dates back centuries to a time when towns and cities were enclosed by defensive walls. It has long been common for a townhouse to have as many as five storeys, depending on its period and grandeur, and from the early 18th century until the late 19th century, most townhouses increased their square footage by extending below street level. When designing a country house, you could put servants, with their tasks of food production and laundry, in a separate wing. In a townhouse, you hid them in the basement, an arrangement that also allowed for a separate tradesmen's entrance and a coal-hole. This was 'below stairs' territory, the domain of the cook and the scullery maid.

The houses in this book have not been chosen as a representative selection of periods or architectural types of English townhouse, but purely for the strength and visual appeal of their decoration. The earliest dates from 1670, the most modern from 1965; five are in London, eight in provincial towns and cities. All, bar two that are semi-detached, are terraced. And all are tall. None stands less than three floors above road level, three have five floors, and nine have lower ground floors originally designed to house the kitchen.

What to do with this old-fashioned arrangement, now that the kitchen is the family hub, is a familiar townhouse dilemma. Do you stay true to an outmoded layout, or do you acknowledge the modern pre-eminence of the kitchen by fitting out a former reception room with oven, dishwasher, refrigerator, and all the paraphernalia of contemporary cuisine? If your kitchen is in the basement, it can be a long way up two or three flights of stairs to find a sweater or the phone you left in a pocket. The in-between reception rooms can become 'dead' space, bypassed en route from a convivial meal with family and friends to bath and bed.

I took to counting stairs. At the top of the league, with the most number of steps from its basement to its attic bedrooms, is John and Louise Stannard's 17th-century, semi-detached London house, with a grand total of 67 (see pages 110–123). Next in line is Frank Hollmeyer's elegant late-18th century house, which has a staircase of 58 steps (see pages 98–109). While John and Louise have made a ground-floor reception room into their kitchen, leaving the basement as a party space, Frank has kept his kitchen on the lower ground floor, where it would always have been, and has chosen to have two floors of receptions rooms. As a result, John and Louise have 35 steps between bed and breakfast, and Frank has 45. Gavin Waddell in Cheltenham (see pages 60–73) and David Campbell and Anita Evagora in York (see pages 22–35) also have ground-floor kitchens in former reception rooms, while Lucy Bathurst built a whole new kitchen at this level, directly above an old scullery extension (see pages 124–135). But Catherine de Moncan and William Roth, who are both retired, recently decided to move their ground-floor kitchen down a level, and have a bedroom at the very top of their four-storey early 18th-century home (see pages 8–21). 'It's good exercise,' William says.

Vertical living is the price you pay for all the advantages of urban infrastructure and culture – pavements and parks, cafés and restaurants, theatres and museums, shops – and for the privilege of your own front door onto the street, your own back garden, however small, and your own patch of territory from ground to sky without other households above or below, or both. Stairs are the inevitable corollary, and the higher your ceilings and the bigger your house, the more of them there will be. Something to remember as you climb your way up the old Apples and Pears to find your phone.

A HUMBLE ELEGANCE

OVER THE LAST THREE CENTURIES, LONDON HAS VASTLY EXPANDED. IN 1715 THE POPULATION WAS 630,000. TODAY IT IS OVER 8 MILLION. SO IT IS THAT A NARROW-FRONTED, EARLY 18TH-CENTURY TERRACED HOUSE, WITH TWO SMALL ROOMS AND A REAR CLOSET ON EACH OF ITS FOUR FLOORS, ONCE THE VILLAGE HOME OF A BUILDER WORKING ON THE CONSTRUCTION OF NEARBY KENSINGTON PALACE, IS TODAY A TROPHY PROPERTY IN A PRIME LOCATION.

Inevitably, this discrepancy between the modest origins of a house and its current status can result in a clash of styles; swagged silk curtains, boulle cabinets, and gilded overmantels lording it over rooms with cottage proportions; the decorating equivalent of mutton dressed as lamb. After careful thought, the owners of this house decided to do it differently.

William Roth and Catherine de Moncan are both French – she a successful artist, he publisher for a group of trade magazines, now retired, and it was his work that brought them to London some 20 years ago. 'In France we lived in an apartment with very big rooms, and high ceilings,' he says. 'Our furniture was Louis XV and Louis XVI, and most of it wouldn't even fit through this front door. Our friends were astonished that we had chosen to buy somewhere so modest. But we loved the early Georgian atmosphere, and we squeezed in what we could of our French furniture and lived here for a couple of years without changing anything.'

ABOVE AND BELOW LEFT *The front door opens into a narrow staircase hall, with a door on the left into the dining room. There is a view along the crooked wooden floor and panelled walls into the music room extension, its rectilinear modernity in striking contrast with the warped and weathered house it is attached to.*

OPPOSITE *When William and Catherine bought the house, the two ground-floor rooms had been opened up to make a single room. With the help of Robert and Josyane Young of Rivière Interiors, a division has been reinstated incorporating cupboards and shelves for the display of creamware platters.*

OPPOSITE *The front room of the basement is the original kitchen, but had more recently been relegated to plant room and storage. It has now reverted to its former use, the old range restored and hand-built fitted cupboards painted in a soft, distressed shade of dirty pink installed.*

LEFT *These stairs lead down from the back of the entrance hall where the glass extension allows light to flood in through the open door that once led into the garden. The floors on this level have been lowered to give better ceiling height, and there is a guest bedroom and bathroom behind the kitchen, both of which look out onto a tiny sunken courtyard afforded by the L-shaped floor plan of the glass extension.*

BELOW *Every inch of available storage space has been utilized, including the vault under the pavement, once used for the delivery and storage of coal. Here, behind an old planked door, is the wine cellar, the freezer, and bikes belonging to William and Catherine's grandchildren, all of whom live in London.*

The owners they bought from had returned the house to domesticity after many years of use as the local post office. They had stripped all the painted panelling and built a conservatory-style room over the little courtyard garden. 'The house had lost something of its period feel,' says William. 'The longer we lived here, the more we wanted to reclaim it, and the more unsuitable our furnishings seemed.'

One day, William was exploring London and came across Robert Young's antiques shop on Battersea Bridge Road. He loved the early country antiques and folk art, and he and Catherine became regular customers. Robert remembers his first impressions. 'They were very quiet and polite,' he says, 'And very discerning. I was delighted, and not a little surprised when they asked if we might help them with their house.'

Robert and his wife Josyane only take on a small number of interior-decorating projects. 'We like to be sure that our ideas and aesthetic are right for a house and its owners,' says Robert. Prolonged discussions with Catherine and William confirmed that they shared an appreciation for patina and the offbeat charm of things handmade by craftsmen for everyday use. They also shared a dislike of 'over-restoration' and agreed that this was an aspect of the house that needed to be addressed.

THIS PAGE AND OPPOSITE *Behind the ground-floor dining room is a small sitting room. A door next to the corner fireplace opens into one of the rooms of the original 'closet wing', a room that William and Catherine used as their kitchen until they remodelled the kitchen in the basement. On the wall on the left of this door is an old speaking tube, dating from when the house was the local post office.*

LEFT AND ABOVE *With its panelling painted a mottled, pale grey in a matt chalky finish, its simple drape of muslin above the windows, and its plain, 18th-century country furnishings, the dining room has a chaste, Gustavian elegance. Catherine's collection of brightly painted French pottery is slightly at odds with this simplicity, but only revealed when the doors of the corner cupboard are flung open. The floor slopes markedly.*

Pegged, nailed, and jointed, as if it were itself a particularly large piece of early 18th-century furniture, the interior structure of the house is entirely made from wood – the external and party walls inside are clad in fielded panelling and rooms are divided by panelled wooden partitions. Floors and staircase are also wood, as are doors, window frames, and shutters. Already crooked when it was first built in 1710, on a plot that is at a slight angle to the road, over three hundred years of occupation, changing weather and moisture levels, pollution and the vibrations of traffic and pneumatic drills, the wooden framework of the house has slowly, gently warped and flexed. Floors slope, window frames sag, door frames droop, and walls curve, in a way that expresses the passing of time more eloquently than any 'historic' decorating scheme ever could. The wood moves, and as it does it talks; the boards squeak and croak underfoot, and in quiet moments you can hear the click

OPPOSITE *Panelling throughout the house has been painted in a special mix, applied such that it looks like original paint that has worn and weathered with time. Colours were chosen for each room after much discussion, here a watery blue-grey. With the door to the landing standing open (opposite), you can see the only piece of grand French furniture William and Catherine kept, a small corner cupboard. To the left is the staircase and to the right the door into the drawing room.*

ABOVE AND ABOVE RIGHT

Behind the drawing room on the first floor is a room they still call the 'music room', as it is the room where William practised his cello when Catherine's painting studio was in the former conservatory extension at the back of the house, now replaced with the new glass extension that is home to a grand piano. Furnishings are a mixture of French and English country pieces, including a painted day bed and a mahogany chest of drawers. The door next to the corner fireplace leads into a small room in the closet wing, now a bathroom.

of a joint shifting in its socket, or a plank settling back into place like the creaking of a wooden ship resting at anchor.

Robert's first suggestion was to repaint walls and panelling in a chalky finish that looks as though it has been revealed from under later layers. The fitted carpets were removed, and missing floorboards were replaced. 'Nothing happened quickly,' says Robert. 'We tackled the house one room at a time – suggesting paint colours, and finding furniture.' Gradually marquetry was swapped for painted deal and country oak, bergères for Windsor chairs, and commodes for chests of drawers, as the glossy sophistication of 18th-century France made way for a humbler aesthetic.

The finished house has a distinctly Gustavian feel, its woodwork in shades of grey, its floorboards

bleached, and its simple 18th-century furnishings all reminiscent of that pared-back version of neoclassicism that Sweden's King Gustav III popularized after his visit to Versailles. Simple, and also neat as a pin – there are no untidy corners, no accumulations or massed collections, just a graceful grouping of Delftware jars on a side table in the first-floor drawing room, and well-spaced cream platters on the dining-room shelves. The only paintings are delicate, ethereal portraits and still lifes by Catherine, which hang from discreet picture rails, and are regularly changed and moved. 'This is how they live,' says Robert, with a mix of awe and admiration.

Two years ago, Catherine and William commissioned architect Oliver Perceval to replace the existing extension, which Catherine was using as a studio, with a glass-walled room,

THIS PAGE *The first-floor drawing room has three windows onto the street. Behind its shutters they found fragments of 19th-century newspaper and pieces of old wallpaper, just some of many traces of past lives in a house that has seen Kensington change beyond recognition from a village to one of the most expensive areas in central London. The coffee table with its zinc top is from Rivière Interiors.*

ABOVE LEFT *In the room behind the bedroom on the top floor of the house, an antique pond yacht sails across the top of an 18th-century tallboy chest of drawers. There are no fitted carpets anywhere in the house. Many of the original floorboards had survived, and those that were missing were replaced with reclaimed boards. Here they have been painted; in other rooms they are bare wood. In all rooms they slope in one direction or another, and creak gently underfoot.*

LEFT *At the top of the stairs on the landing outside the main bedroom is a painted desk. Above it, and a little further down the stairs, hang two paintings by Catherine. Throughout the house pictures are suspended from discreet rails where wall and ceiling meet, such that they can be easily moved or replaced. Running up the right hand of the stairs is a sloping fitted cupboard with a hinged lid, which may have been used to store coal for the upstairs fireplaces.*

leaving just enough outdoor space for stone steps up to a terrace on its flat roof. Catherine has found another studio a few streets away, and this bright, clean space has become the music room, where William's cello is propped next to a grand piano. The contrast between the wonky, weathered house and this glassy, rectilinear add-on could not be more extreme.

The new extension prompted a reordering of space. The kitchen, which had been tucked into the closet off the back room on the ground floor,

was moved down to its original place in the basement. Robert designed cupboards with curved corners, and the Victorian range was restored. There is a larder in the space under the entrance hall, and wine racks and grandchildren's bicycles in the vault beneath the pavement; there is a cupboard by the kitchen door for the ironing board and vacuum cleaner, and the washing machine and dryer are secreted under the stairs. Every inch of space is used and everything has its place. 'It's a very calm house,' says Robert.

ABOVE *In the main bedroom, the extent to which the floor slopes is evident in the height of the wooden blocks under the front legs of the chest of drawers, required to ensure that its top is level. The panelling and fitted cupboard are original, but the early Georgian fireplace has been embellished with later additions and fitted with an early Victorian register grate. A flower painting by Catherine hangs above the mantelpiece.*

STUDIO PORTRAIT

WHEN ARTIST DAVID CAMPBELL HOSTS AN OPEN STUDIO WEEKEND, HE IS SOMETIMES ASKED WHAT COLOUR HE AND HIS WIFE ANITA EVAGORA ARE PLANNING TO PAINT THEIR WALLS. THE SPACE WHERE HE CREATES HIS LAYERED AND TACTILE CANVASES IS THE FRONT ROOM OF THEIR MID-VICTORIAN TERRACED HOUSE IN YORK. EVEN WHEN CLEARED AND ARRANGED FOR VISITORS, THE SHEETS OF CARDBOARD THAT USUALLY CARPET THE FLOOR FOLDED AWAY, PICTURES PRICED AND LINED UP ON BENCHES OR HUNG ON THE WALLS, THIS GRACIOUS, HIGH-CEILINGED ROOM HAS A RAW WORKMANLIKE FEEL. DAVID BUILDS COLOUR AND TEXTURE USING A VARIETY OF MATERIALS AND PIGMENTS, FROM GESSO MADE WITH RABBIT-SKIN GLUE, TO BEESWAX, SOOT, RUST, SAND, AND BITUMEN, SO IT IS HARDLY SURPRISING IF THE FITTED DRAWERS AND CUPBOARDS, AND THE WORN GREY LINOLEUM ARE SPATTERED AND STAINED. IT SEEMS ENTIRELY PRACTICAL TO HAVE LEFT THE WALLS OF THIS ROOM UNPAINTED.

ABOVE LEFT *At the foot of the stairs in the entrance hall hangs one of David Campbell's densely layered mixed-media paintings, its subject, like all his art, inspired by the natural world. A tree branch, painted matt white and suspended on the wall, points the way up to the next floor.*

BELOW LEFT *The antique glass of a mirror in the entrance hall reflects soft, sooty images of the door into David's studio at the front of the*

house, and beyond it, the door into the kitchen at the back. A line-up of vintage alarm clocks stands in front of ranked family photographs.

OPPOSITE *Another of David's paintings hangs above the high kitchen table, the base of which came from York University, while the top, like the fitted cupboards to its right, was rescued from the pavement when London's Camden School for Girls refurbished its science laboratories.*

However, visitors will notice that the walls of the staircase hall, and of the kitchen, are similarly undressed, their old lime plaster mottled by time and marked where holes and cracks have been filled. If they were invited upstairs to the drawing room and adjacent bedroom, they would see that this undecorated aesthetic continues, at which point they might realize that it must be intentional, not just a case of terminal indecision. 'Stripping the walls was a labour of love,' says David. 'The whole house was papered with woodchip. I spent days and months steaming it off. I rigged up a plumbing pipe so that I could wedge the steamer in place, and carry on scraping while the steamer did its work.'

It's a big house, on four floors, with big rooms – two or three to a floor. That's a lot of woodchip. And steaming was not the only laborious task. Anita rubbed down every turned banister rail from the basement to the attic to get rid of the lumpy layers of gloss paint. Under the fitted carpets they found original floorboards and David set himself the task of filling every gap with slivers of wood, cut, hammered into place, and sanded. Stained dark ebony, the floors are now seamless, and splinter free. Woodwork is painted grey – a shade they mixed themselves. Stripped of the padding and distractions of carpeting, colour, and pattern, the handsome and robust mid-1850s architecture of the house is laid bare, its pleasing proportions, simple cornices/crown moldings, deep skirtings/baseboards, and plain architraves all accentuated.

LEFT *The kitchen is entirely fitted with reclaimed cupboards, drawers, and shelves, including the stainless steel sink unit – unseen to the right under the window onto the garden – which was from a biology laboratory in York University. Here, as in the hall seen through the door, and in much of the rest of the house, the old lime plaster dating from when the house was built in the mid-19th century has been left stripped bare of later paint and wallpaper, and shows the scars where holes have been made for various fittings over the years. Old blue and white china is stacked on the open shelves ready for use.*

Sixteen years ago when they first saw the house, it was the architecture that sold it to them. 'At the time we were living in a two-bedroom flat in Camden,' says Anita, 'in the house where I was brought up. I was working incredibly hard running Fred Bare with my partner Carolyn Brookes-Davies. We sold our hats all over the world, had shops in London; it was full-on. David and I decided we needed more space, and a different way of life. The children were five and ten and we began by looking for Quaker schools outside London. There was a school we liked the look of in York.

I had never been before, but David's grandfather came from York, and his parents live in Swaledale. We visited for a day and I was really taken by the city – it is so beautifully preserved, and people are very friendly and good-natured – and we loved the school. We viewed three or four properties before we saw this – speculatively, because it was more than we could afford. But when we got to the first floor, and stood in the room at the front with its three windows, I said to David "we have to buy this house". We made a low offer, and luckily it was accepted.'

OPPOSITE *David's studio moved up into the ground-floor front reception room when they made the lower ground floor, where he had previously worked, into a separate flat. A door, surrounded by a mosaic of photographs of textures and surfaces, buildings and landscapes, connects the room with the kitchen. The thick book on the bench with marbled edges is an old solicitor's ledger David has used as a sketchbook.*

RIGHT *David surrounds himself with inspiration, including his own photographs, postcards of favourite paintings, and pressed and dried plants, here an anemone taped to the wall above the fireplace and poppy seed heads piled on the mantelpiece.*

PAGES 28–29 *When we photographed David's studio it had been tidied and arranged ready for a York Open Studios weekend, when several hundred people are likely to visit over two days. More usually the floor is covered in sheets of cardboard, flattened from the boxes that bicycles are packed in. The room is a studio and also something of an artist's laboratory where David experiments with pigments and materials, variously using gesso made with rabbit-skin glue, beeswax, bitumen, and even coal dust and rust to create the surface textures of his paintings.*

Initially, Anita continued running Fred Bare, had a millinery workshop in the basement, and commuted to London three days a week. In 2008, she and Carolyn decided to close down the business, at which point David took over the basement as his studio. More recently, David moved his studio upstairs and they converted the basement into a separate flat, installing a kitchen and dividing the living room from the bedroom with a wall of elegantly proportioned glazed and panelled doors salvaged from a chateau – a lucky find from The French House that just happened to fit the space perfectly. Here the walls are painted white, and there is new flooring in wide planks of oak. Light and spacious, with a big antique bed, and linen-covered sofa, the apartment gets booked up well in advance.

ABOVE *The lower ground floor is light and spacious and has been turned into a stylish, self-contained flat for holiday lets. Dividing the bedroom from the living room is a wall of antique glazed and panelled doors, salvaged from a chateau. They fitted the space to within an inch and came from The French House in exchange for one of David's paintings.*

LEFT *On the first floor at the front of the house is a large room with three windows looking across the street to the houses and trees opposite. Despite the fitted carpets, and the flock wallpaper, this one room convinced them they should buy the house. As in the hall, having stripped off the wallpaper, they have left the plaster bare, and lines of filler above the piano mark out where pipes for the gas lighting once ran. The chandelier over the table is one of David's creations, and incorporates a metal pineapple found at a car boot/yard sale. The painting of cows on the far wall is by David's great-grandfather, the celebrated Swiss artist Eugène Burnand.*

OPPOSITE *A sofa and chairs upholstered in their original green chenille, bought at auction, are gathered around the fireplace. The green velvet curtains were purchased from Greenwich Market, and the rugs picked up 'for nothing', also from local auctions.*

The French doors are not the only discarded fittings and furnishings to have found a new home. David and Anita were early adopters of the upcycling that has become so fashionable, just as they were ahead of their time when they decided not to paint their stripped plaster. The kitchen has wooden drawers, cabinets, and work surfaces that Anita spotted outside Camden School for Girls when the science laboratories were being refurbished. 'We kept it all wrapped up in our garden in London, knowing we would be able to use it at some stage,' she says. Scratched school-girl graffiti – 'Bowie lives on' and 'Jean's last biology lesson' – are relics of its former life. The big stainless steel sink used to inhabit a biology lab at York University.

OPPOSITE *The main bedroom is on the second floor and has an antique brass bedstead facing an overmantel propped against the wall. One of the birthday necklaces David makes for Anita from found pieces such as the stems of old clay pipes hangs on a smaller mirror.*

RIGHT AND BELOW *Since leaving school to go to university, their daughter has moved to a larger bedroom behind the sitting room on the first floor, and has decorated the wall above her bed with a fan of favourite images. The shell-encrusted mirror on her dressing table (right) is by Anita's former business partner Carolyn Brookes-Davies.*

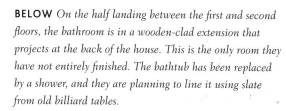

BELOW *On the half landing between the first and second floors, the bathroom is in a wooden-clad extension that projects at the back of the house. This is the only room they have not entirely finished. The bathtub has been replaced by a shower, and they are planning to line it using slate from old billiard tables.*

LEFT *There are two bedrooms at the front on the second floor. Looking through the door of this one, with its surround of bookshelves, there is a view across the landing and down a flight of stairs to the bathroom. Here, as elsewhere in the house, the old floorboards have been meticulously restored by David, and stained black. The grey of the paintwork on the stairs and the landing is a colour they mixed themselves.*

OPPOSITE *When the family first moved to York, the children were six and ten. David painted the walls of his daughter's bedroom with her favourite flowers, including roses, honeysuckle, and hollyhocks. The antique bedstead, bought from The French House, was one of their first purchases for the house, and the light above the bed is another of David's concoctions, hung with nuggets of copper ore found in the Yorkshire Dales and a dried pomegranate.*

Upstairs, in the room that sold them the house, where three windows look across the wide street to the brick gables of the facing terrace and the garden trees that rise behind them, the chandelier is another example of creative reuse, combining a metal pineapple found at a car boot/yard sale and the branches of an antique oil lamp, from which David has hung clear glass balls. On the floor above, another light fitting is constructed from salvaged metal and adorned with a dried pomegranate and nuggets of copper ore, found by David and Anita near an abandoned copper mine in the Yorkshire Dales. David even makes his own canvases using army tarpaulin, purchased years ago as part of a project he was involved in, designing and building the sets for a video for the band ABC.

David and Anita first met as students at London's Royal College of Art. Anita studied Ceramics and, now that the house is nearly finished and the holiday let is up and running, she has started making coil pots again, and firing them in a kiln in the garden. Creativity runs in the family, and is apparent everywhere – a fan of photographs pasted onto the plaster over their daughter Mimi's bed; an eccentric wall light in the main bedroom, constructed from old chair legs, with battered brass knobs as finials; the 'birthday' necklaces, draped over a mirror, made by David for Anita from the broken stems of clay pipes and adorned with tiny glass bottles containing photographs of the children. 'It's all of a piece,' says David. 'The art, and the house, the house and the art.'

A FAMILY TRADITION

ON HIS INSTAGRAM ACCOUNT, GARDENER AND ANTIQUE DEALER JACK LAVER BRISTER CALLS HIMSELF 'TRADCHAP'. HE CAN'T REMEMBER EXACTLY HOW HE CAME UP WITH THIS MONIKER. 'I JUST THOUGHT IT WAS CATCHY,' HE SAYS, 'AND I AM QUITE TRADITIONAL, BUT NOT IN A STUFFY WAY.' HIS DIMINUTIVE, END-OF-TERRACE 1780S HOUSE IN THE SMALL MARKET TOWN OF FROME, IS FURNISHED WITH ANTIQUES TYPICAL OF THE ENGLISH COUNTRY HOUSE, ITS SASH WINDOWS HUNG WITH CURTAINS IN FRAYED SILK DAMASK AND OLD GLAZED CHINTZ. JACK COLLECTS 18TH- AND EARLY 19TH-CENTURY CHINA, AND HAS AN EYE FOR LARGE PORTRAITS OF THE ANCESTRAL VARIETY. THERE ARE STAFFORDSHIRE DOGS STANDING ON THE DINING ROOM MANTELPIECE, AND GERANIUMS ON THE WINDOWSILLS.

ABOVE LEFT *Wreathed in wisteria, the front door with its canopied porch is more cottage than townhouse, even though the steps lead straight to the pavement. The terrace of houses continues to the right of the front door, but ends abruptly to its left, where the adjoining house was demolished to give access to later buildings behind.*

LEFT *The front door opens into a staircase hall painted in Farrow & Ball's Railings – a grey so dark, it is almost black. There are two ground-floor reception rooms opening off to the right of the hall.*

OPPOSITE *This, the back room, is painted dark brown (Farrow & Ball's London Clay) and furnished with a few of the mid-century modern pieces favoured by Richard. The red armchair on the right was one of many made to a design by Lord Snowdon for the investiture of The Prince of Wales in 1969 and is, says Jack, very uncomfortable. The Poole Pottery vase on the table was bought at a car boot/yard sale, and the large piece of David Hicks carpet was retrieved from a skip/dumpster.*

What is less traditional is that this is the home of a man only just out of his twenties. If you were to meet Jack and his partner Richard Nares in a pub, you might guess that they were going back to in a flat in Stepney with IKEA shelves and a serious sound system. Richard admits to a liking for mid-century modern, but Jack's decorating heroes are John Fowler and David Mlinaric.

They both love old houses. Richard is a conservation building surveyor, and Jack comes from a long line of West Country auctioneers and antiques dealers – his parents have an antiques shop near Somerton. 'We saw the particulars for this house online, more than a year before we bought it. It was our dream house – near the centre of town, and with all its period features,'

OPPOSITE *Although it is the same diminutive size as the back living room, the living room at the front retains the feel of a 'best' room, with its marbled fireplace, dado/chair rail, and cornice/crown molding. As well as several large pieces of antique furniture, it is home to some of Jack's extensive collection of late 18th- and early 19th-century china, displayed on original fitted shelving to the right of the fireplace.*

LEFT *Standing with your back to the fireplace, there is a view into the entrance hall, where a section of 19th-century French panelling with an integral mirror reflects the room, and the sitting room behind it. Jack and Richard have resisted the temptation to knock these rooms through, reasoning that they would lose precious wall space if they did. The matting rug is from IKEA.*

ABOVE *The glazed bureau-bookcase was inherited from Jack's grandfather. Squeezed between it and the display cabinet on the left of the fireplace is one of a pair of early Victorian Gothic chairs.*

says Richard. As is so often the case with dream houses, its price was slightly out of reach. But it didn't sell, despite its charm, so when eventually they decided to make an offer, it was accepted.

Before the previous owner modernized, the basement had been used as a lawnmower workshop, a fate that probably helped to preserve its old fittings. Jack and Richard were delighted to find the brackets with eyelets through which bell wires were threaded still in place in the ceilings. 'It's amazing to think that people in a house like this would have had a servant,' says Jack. Other relics of a past when labour was plentiful and cheap are the brick copper water heater in the corner of the basement front room and, next to

it, a cast-iron range, complete with its tap/faucet: 'hot water and a washing machine – all mod cons'.

Richard and Jack use this room as a dining room, and the original scullery has been knocked through and is now the kitchen. On the floor above, the two reception rooms have fireplaces that seem disproportionately large. The front room, always the 'best' room, is further embellished by dado/chair and picture rails. Up another flight of stairs and there is a bedroom at the front and a smaller bathroom at the back. Up again, and there is an attic bedroom. It's ideal accommodation for two, but slightly cramped by modern standards for a family and children, plus servant.

LEFT *The basement was originally two rooms, a kitchen at the front and a scullery at the back. These have been knocked into one and the scullery is now the kitchen, leading into a dining room just seen to the left of this image. The dresser/hutch is crammed with old china, and the wall cupboard is antique but was badly damaged, so Jack painted it a vibrant buttercup yellow.*

ABOVE *To the left of the fireplace in the dining room is the old built-in brick copper, complete with a wooden 'dolly' for stirring the washing.*

OPPOSITE *The kitchen has one small, high window onto the rear courtyard. A strategically placed mirror propped in the rebate helps to reflect more light into the room.*

Although the house retained much of its original fabric, some of the period atmosphere had been dampened by white paint and wall-to-wall carpeting. The first thing they did on moving in was to ditch the carpet. Underneath, the floorboards prickled with nails and staples, and in some places were tacky with tar-like glue that had been used to stick down linoleum. There were also faded lines of wood stain marking out where, over the years, rugs had been placed. Nails, staples, and tar had to go, but they left the rug shadows. 'I like that lived-in, worn look that reveals the history of a room,' says Jack.

With his knowledge of antiques, Jack takes responsibility for furnishings – many of which he found by trawling through eBay, and also at markets and from auctions. He is adept at spotting and rescuing things. The carved oak side table that has been converted to make a base for the bathroom washbasin was covered in thick white gloss paint

OPPOSITE *The old kitchen has come up in the world since the days when the copper in the corner and the old cast-iron range in the fireplace were in use. It is now the dining room, and full of the kind of furniture, paintings, and china that would once have been found in more formal rooms. The 18th-century corner cupboard, with its pretty fretwork and shaped shelves still with their original coat of green paint, was found by Jack on eBay.*

ABOVE *Although below street level at the front, the basement leads out to a tiny courtyard because the house is set on a slope. This outdoor space may be short on sunlight, but Jack has used his gardening skills to make it lush as a jungle.*

RIGHT *Looking across the end of the dining table, and past the old planked door with its metal latch, to the original stone flooring of the basement passage, worn to a shine by generations of feet.*

ABOVE *The old pine table is almost the only piece of furniture that would once have been at home in this basement kitchen. Chairs are a selection of mismatched 18th-century dining chairs, and the low-hanging chandelier and silver candlesticks are far too grand for such a humble space. Inappropriate though they are, the effect of this mix of the formal and informal, the rustic and the sophisticated, is charming.*

and had been dumped in a recycling centre, and the piece of David Hicks carpet in the ground-floor back room was found in a skip/dumpster. Gardening, which is Jack's work four days a week, has also proved decoratively fruitful. The yellow silk curtains in the bedroom were being thrown out by one of his clients because their leading edges had shredded due to sun damage. Jack turned them and now the damaged edges hang like intricately slashed Tudor sleeves at the outer ends of the curtain pole.

Wear and tear is welcomed. Much of the china is cracked, chipped, or mended. 'I couldn't afford such nice stuff if I bought it perfect,' says Jack. 'And I love the old mends where they have used metal rivets. It shows that a piece was treasured.' Nor is he averse to cobbling things together or chopping them up. The kitchen dresser/hutch is a 'marriage' of two separate pieces, and the 18th-century linen press in the dining room has had its back removed so that it sits in front of the gas and electricity meters and fuse box and hides them. The walnut veneer wardrobe in the main bedroom had to be sawn in half in order to get it up the stairs.

OPPOSITE *To the right of the fireplace is an original fitted cupboard that now displays a set of early 19th-century Mason's Ironstone plates and two particularly fine lustre jugs. There is more lustre on the mantelpiece, flanked by a pair of large Staffordshire dogs. The Victorian range, complete with its hot water tap/faucet, and the copper probably survived because these rooms were used as a workshop for some years in the last century and so escaped modernization. In the foreground is another chair from the Investiture of The Prince of Wales.*

Richard's contribution is colour. His choices are subtle, and contribute to the slightly Dickensian feel of this old-fashioned, urban cottage. The hall and stairs are dark grey, almost black – counter-intuitive for these confined spaces that are already short on natural light. 'The darkness makes a great foil for all the pictures,' he says, 'and I think it also gives an illusion of space.' In the bedroom, a very soft, shell pink is offset by woodwork in a neutral tone halfway between grey and khaki 'in order to knock back the prettiness of the pink'. The front room is in the same neutral, the back room rich brown. Only the basement rooms and ceilings are still white.

Dark colours give an illusion of space and, as any professional decorator will tell you, so do large pieces of furniture – of which there are several, including the basement linen press, and the bedroom wardrobe. Big pieces help to ballast all the smaller stuff, and are crucial to the balance of rooms that are as full as these. Strategically placed mirrors also play their light- and space-expanding part, not just the ground-floor overmantels, but a mirror in the rebate of the small kitchen window that nearly doubles the light, and a section of French mirrored panelling placed in the hall such that it reflects a view into both front and back rooms. It won't be long before someone asks Jack to help them decorate their house – and perhaps Richard will chip in with ideas for paint colours.

PAGES 46–47 *This first-floor bedroom is bigger than either reception room, as it spans the front of the house. Richard chose the colour scheme, a soft pink for the walls (Setting Plaster by Farrow & Ball), matched with a sludgy grey-green (Farrow & Ball's Mouse's Back) for woodwork 'to knock back the prettiness'. The bed head and hangings are in vintage chintz by GP and J Baker, bought at auction. Through the door there is a view of the stairs leading up to the single attic bedroom, the decoration of which is currently a work in progress.*

ABOVE LEFT *A glazed cabinet on the bathroom wall opposite the washbasin has an interior painted the same pink as the adjacent bedroom and holds a collection of shells and coral.*

LEFT *This is the only room in the house with wallpaper: 'Raphael' by Sandberg. 'We thought we could allow ourselves to be a bit more wacky in here,' says Jack. Contributing to the wackiness are second-hand glazed chintz curtains, and a sample of scarlet Axminster carpet, old stock from an interior-decorating shop. The gilded chair with its carved crest has been stripped of its upholstery fabric, showing the construction of its buttoned, horsehair seat.*

OPPOSITE *Jack found the carved oak base of the washbasin in a recycling centre, coated with thick white gloss paint. He already had a piece of old marble, which was cut to fit the top.*

THE BEST DEAL

IN 1660, SAMUEL PEPYS DESCRIBED THE TOWN OF DEAL ON THE COAST OF KENT AS 'PITIFUL'. IT HADN'T IMPROVED BY 1823, WHEN WILLIAM COBBETT CALLED IT 'A MOST VILLAINOUS PLACE ... FULL OF FILTHY-LOOKING PEOPLE'. SPEED THROUGH ANOTHER TWO CENTURIES, AND THE PICTURE IS VERY DIFFERENT. STREETS THAT WERE ONCE SEEDY AND IMPOVERISHED HAVE BEEN TIDIED AND SMARTENED, SASH WINDOWS RESTORED, DOORS PAINTED, AND THE HIGH STREET HAS WON A NATIONAL AWARD. SOLDIERS, SAILORS, AND MINERS HAVE BEEN REPLACED BY ARTY 'DFLs' (DOWN FROM LONDON) BRINGING CASH AND DIFFERENT PRIORITIES TO THIS ANCIENT 'CINQUE PORT' TOWN.

Kathryn and Jonathan Reilly moved here in 2013, and say they already feel they have always lived here. 'We have more local friends than we have ever had – there's a strong community and we are part of it. It's a slower way of life, so there is time to talk to people you meet on the street, to get to know your neighbours and get involved in local issues.' Jonathan is a director of the antiquarian bookseller Maggs, so commutes to London four days a week, but Kathryn, who is a writer and digital editor, works from home, and

OPPOSITE *The house has a cellar, but no basement, and the kitchen is at the back, its windows overlooking the walled garden. The antique table has a top made from a single piece of oak. 'We were so excited about the house and what we were going to do to it, we bought the table for this room before we had even completed on the purchase,' says Kathryn.*

ABOVE RIGHT *A cooker now sits in the recess of the original 18th-century*

kitchen fireplace, and above it hangs some of Kathryn's collection of antique wooden spoons.

RIGHT *Next to the door that leads from the entrance hall into the kitchen is a glazed storage cupboard that Kathryn bought from Deal-based interior decorator Martin Wharton, when he had a shop on the high street. 'We did a swap,' says Kathryn. 'I designed his website and he gave me the cupboard in exchange.'*

OPPOSITE *The front door opens into a narrow hall with the staircase ahead and, at its foot, the door into the kitchen. This is the front of the two ground-floor rooms, a library and sitting room, with two sash windows looking onto the street. Fitted bookshelves on opposing walls hold some of Jonathan's collection of books, and the original early 18th-century pine panelling is painted the dark grey of a stormy sea.*

ABOVE LEFT *A pair of vintage leather club chairs faces the fireplace while a procession of vintage toy dogs sets off across the floor from behind one of them.*

ABOVE *To the left of the fireplace is an original fitted cupboard, its shaped shelves painted kingfisher blue – a splash of brilliant colour that immediately attracts the eye to their intriguing contents, which include a line-up of even smaller dogs, knitted, carved, felted, and stuffed. The room and the shelves are reflected in a group of convex mirrors hanging on the adjacent wall.*

her office is an old smokehouse in the garden. She has already made a name for herself in Deal by self-publishing a book of her photographs entitled *Dogs of Deal*. More recent is *Behind Closed Doors*, again photographed and written by Kathryn and proof that Deal is unusually rich in pretty period houses with stylish interiors.

It was one of these that first brought her to the town to write about decorator Martin Wharton of design company Settle, his house and his shop Mileage, for *Coast* magazine. 'We were living in Hertfordshire but keen to move, as there were plans for a large new housing estate in the field next to our house. I was going to interview Martin on the phone, but it was a grey February day and I decided to drive down and

meet him in person. Even in drizzle, I loved the town. When I suggested to Jonathan that we should look at houses there, I thought he would blow me out of the water because the commute was so much longer. But he didn't rule it out and said that his criteria were good fish and chips, a nice pub, and a baker. Deal has them all, so we tried catching the train from London one day after work, and realized it was a nice journey.'

This was the fourth house they viewed. 'How could we resist?' says Kathryn. 'A Georgian house, literally yards from the sea – it seemed almost too good to be true.' What she is too polite to say, but is revealed by a glance at the estate agent's particulars, is that the interior was relentlessly bland, its period charm smothered

pretty rooms. They made the ground-floor front room a library lined with shelves that hold and display Jonathan's books, many with handsome bindings. They took out the kitchen island and put in a table with a top crafted from a single plank of oak. They made up for the loss of kitchen cupboards with an antique glazed cabinet from Martin Wharton's shop, which Kathryn paid for by designing a website for him. Two antique doors that had been mouldering in the cellar made fronts for a wall cupboard over the sink. The old pine panelling was painted again, as it would originally have been, a dark flannel grey in the library, and a paler shade of grey in the living room. Kathryn collected shells from the beach – 'there aren't many in the shingle, so it took a long time' – and when she had enough, she stuck them on the walls of the downstairs lavatory to make what she calls her 'grotty grotto'.

Both Kathryn and Jonathan are collectors – he of books, and also the illustrations and prints of Edward Ardizzone, Eric Ravilious, and Edward Bawden, she of various things from mourning jewellery to vintage toy dogs to milagros – Mexican folk charms. Since they moved, she has started collecting items connected with Deal. So there are ships in bottles, photographs of heroic Victorian lifeboatmen in cork life jackets, shell souvenirs, and a sailor's Valentine.

Kathryn revels in the disreputable past of her new home. 'I was speaking to an old man who has lived in Deal all his life. Apparently, his mother used to tell him not to come to this part of town because it was so rough and dangerous.' The house was the scene of a double murder in the 19th century, and Kathryn thinks at one stage it might have been a brothel. She is tempted to dig out the cellar and see what she can find. 'Deal was renowned for smugglers,' she says. 'Anyone found with contraband in their cellar was obliged to fill it in with rubble. I think that might have happened to this house, as we only have half a cellar.' It is no surprise to learn she is writing a novel – a historical one, of course.

ABOVE *The biggest room is at the front on the first floor, and has two windows overlooking the Georgian terraced houses opposite, and this third window at the side, which looks down the street away from the sea. The old glazed cupboard holds a selection of mantel clocks, pottery, and stuffed birds, among other things.*

OPPOSITE *Two of the doors in the house, that into the kitchen, and this door from the first-floor landing, have hinged glass panes set into them. Kathryn speculates that the house may once have been a brothel, as were many others in this seaside town.*

by fitted carpets and pastel paint, its original panelling stripped, stained ginger, and varnished to look like the interior of a sauna. Kathryn and Jonathan saw past this to the bones of a house that retained its old floorboards, staircase, glazed cupboards, and alcove shelving. Arranged on three floors, it has a kitchen facing south and opening straight into the garden and a living room upstairs with windows onto the street on two sides. Being at the end of a terrace, it also has the luxury of a garage and a wider garden than most of the houses on these narrow streets.

After moving in, they set about recovering the character that had been bleached out of these

PAGES 56–57 *In the first-floor sitting room, the strawberry reds of the sofa, the vintage rug, and the table lamp, and the vibrant forest green of the velvet armchair, positively glow against a background of original fielded and matchboard panelling painted pale grey and off-white. Between the windows, in a vellum frame by Simon Orrell, is a wallpaper design of 1928 by artist Edward Bawden.*

LEFT *On the first-floor landing, the door ahead opens into the front sitting room, and a door on the right into the guest bedroom. The drawing above the bookshelves is by David Gentleman, one of the 20th-century artists and illustrators whose work Jonathan collects.*

BELOW LEFT *Between the kitchen and the back door into the garden, under the slope of the stairs, is a*

downstairs lavatory that Kathryn has encrusted with shells gathered from the beach just down the road. 'It took a year of beachcombing,' she says, 'as it isn't a beach that has many shells.'

BELOW *A windowsill on the stairs, where the steps turn up to the first-floor landing, holds a small fleet of ships in bottles. On the wall are some of the pieces of wood carving they have been collecting as a couple, since they bought their first piece on honeymoon in Venice.*

OPPOSITE *From the glazed right-hand flank of the dormer window in the attic bedroom, there is a view down the narrow street to the sea. Some of Kathryn's extensive collection of Mexican religious charms, or milagros, stud the beam above the bed.*

Fashion Statement

THE ENTRANCE HALL IS DUSTY MAUVE, THE
KITCHEN IS A BOWER OF PINK, BLUE, AND
GREEN FLORAL WALLPAPER, AND THE DOUBLE
DRAWING ROOM, WITH ITS FLOOR-TO-CEILING
SASH WINDOWS, GLOWS BUTTERCUP YELLOW.
THERE IS A TABLE PAINTED CORAL RED; THERE
ARE SOFAS UPHOLSTERED IN BROAD SCARLET
STRIPES. CONFIDENT, UNCONVENTIONAL,
JOYFUL, THESE ARE ROOMS PUT TOGETHER BY
SOMEONE WHO LOVES PATTERN AND COLOUR,
AND KNOWS HOW TO USE THEM.

Gavin Waddell bought this spacious Regency townhouse in
Cheltenham more than 30 years ago. At the time he was head
of fashion at Gloucestershire College of Art and Design, and
had been commuting to work from a cottage in Ross-on-Wye.
He spotted a 'For Sale' sign while driving past the house one
day and booked a viewing, thinking that it looked like 'a nice
little place'. He was wrong on both counts. It was much bigger
than expected, and had been crudely carved up into bedsits.

OPPOSITE AND RIGHT *The
kitchen leads off the staircase hall
opposite the first door to the double
drawing room, and would originally
have been another reception room.
A sink and oven now stand in front
of the chimney breast and fitted
cabinets fill the recesses on either
side. The Cole & Son floral wallpaper
was bought in a sale, together with
almost all the other wallpaper in the
house, and inspired the bright green
of the cabinets and the coral red of
the table. Bamboo shelving, designed
by Gavin, holds blue and white
china ready for use.*

ABOVE RIGHT *The impressive front
door opens into a square entrance hall.
To the right is a door into the staircase
hall, which is enlivened by another
cut-price Cole & Son wallpaper from
the same sale, with a pattern like
geometric tiling. Many of the original
early Victorian features of the house
were intact, if damaged, including
the stone staircase, with its unusual
mahogany banister rail sweeping
seamlessly down to form a newel
post, terminating in a carved lion's
foot. Here, as elsewhere in the house,
the original floorboards have been
restored and polished.*

'There were two communal kitchens, with four stoves in each, posters on the walls, and 1950s tiled fireplaces. It was in a terrible state,' Gavin says, 'but I could see the potential.'

Cheltenham is an elegant town, a smaller, more relaxed version of Bath, developed as a spa throughout the 18th and early 19th centuries after the discovery of mineral springs in 1716. A visit from George III in 1788 bestowed royal cachet. This house was built in 1840; substantial, semi-detached, and part of a curved 'circus' of houses of the same date. Originally there were kitchens and servants' rooms in the basement, four reception rooms on the ground floor, and five bedrooms on the floor above.

Although the fireplaces had gone and rooms had been divided, there was enough of the original fabric to encourage restoration. There were fine cornices/crown moldings and deep skirtings/baseboards, shutters, floorboards, and even some old crown glass in the large-paned sash windows. The stone staircase is a particularly handsome survival, with its mahogany banister rail sweeping down to form a lobed and foliate newel post terminating in a large, stylized lion's foot planted stoutly on the bottom step.

Initially, Gavin directed works from a rented flat just down the road while partition walls were taken down and a wide opening knocked through between the front reception rooms to make a

LEFT *Recessed at one side of the house, the handsome panelled front door opens into this square entrance hall, which is painted the mauve of lilac flowers and furnished with pieces that reflect the date of the house, arranged with classical symmetry. To the right, glazed doors open into the staircase hall, which runs the width of the house parallel to the street, with the two main reception rooms to its right overlooking the front garden.*

OPPOSITE *The end of the double reception room nearest the front door also has a distinctly Regency feel, enhanced by the buttercup yellow of the walls, a 'Chinese' yellow much favoured by decorators of the period. The gilded overmantel reflects the opening between the two rooms and the overmantel at the far end directly opposite. Still life paintings to the left of the chimney breast are by Gavin.*

OPPOSITE When Gavin bought the house it had been carved up into bedsits, and the two front reception rooms were separate, as they would have been when the house was built. He knocked a square opening between them to make a grand, double room, with two generous floor-to-ceiling sash windows. There is a fireplace at either end of the room, each with its complement of seating, here a Regency sofa covered in a contemporary print.

LEFT The elaborate carving of a Jacobean-style 19th-century chair is silhouetted against the white paint of the window shutters at the end of the room with the red striped sofas. Next to it is a Regency pedestal table.

BELOW Behind one of the sofas, two glass vases on a sideboard hold artificial bird of paradise flowers below an 18th-century Venetian mirror. A pair of early Victorian family portraits hangs on either side of the mirror, and to the right is an 18th-century tallboy chest of drawers.

single space spanning the facade. A smaller reception room at the back of the house became his kitchen. He commissioned craftsmen to revive woodwork and replace missing sections of cornice/crown molding, and found chimney pieces in architectural salvage yards. The magnificent 18th-century carved wooden fireplace and overmantel at one end of the drawing room was first bought in pieces by his sister, the interior designer Sasha Waddell, but proved too big for her own house. 'It was coated in white gloss paint, and only cost her £100. It was the wrong period, but I realized as soon as I saw it that it was the right scale for this house,' says Gavin.

Some aspects of the decor were inspired by Regency taste, such as the Chinese yellow of the drawing room, but the dates and styles of the furnishings range widely, from the 17th to the 21st centuries, from Gothic to classical, baroque to Biedermeier – what Gavin calls 'a hotchpotch'. A 'hotchpotch' it may be, but one of unusual flair, which Gavin describes as 'a form of abstract painting in three dimensions'. It isn't everyone who would hang 18th- and 19th-century family portraits on either side of a Chinese scroll painting, or place vases of artificial bird of paradise flowers in front of an 18th-century Venetian mirror, or shocking pink towels and a yellow chair in a bathroom papered in a design of flowering lilac on a black background.

PAGES 66–67 *The magnificent carved chimney piece and overmantel at this end of the drawing room was originally bought by Gavin's sister, interior decorator Sasha Waddell, for her own kitchen. When it proved too large, Gavin was delighted to adopt it, knowing that its scale, if not its date, was right for this room.*

LEFT *The stone staircase continues up a half flight from the first-floor landing to a fourth bedroom. The walls here are hung with fashion drawings by Gavin Waddell, who ran his own couture company for some years, and later had his own label, Geva, in 1969 and also designed for Bellville Sassoon.*

OPPOSITE *There are two large bedrooms at the front of the house, above the double reception room, one of which Gavin made into an elegant upstairs drawing room and study. Walls are a gorgeous blue-green – 'I didn't want a bright turquoise, or a dull one,' says Gavin. 'It took a lot of trial and error to find just the right colour – vibrant and yet receding.' Here, as downstairs, there is a confident mixing of styles, and periods – neoclassical and baroque, oriental and Western, old and new.*

The kitchen is particularly surprising. It must once have been a morning room, and retains its chimney breast and a cornice/crown molding starred with sculpted flower heads. Gavin bought the floral wallpaper in a sale at Cole & Son. Someone less adventurous might have used it in a bedroom, but here it is matched with black and white chequerboard linoleum, a black-tiled splashback, and fitted cupboards painted strong green, for an overall effect that is pretty but also workmanlike. Bamboo shelves display blue and white Spode plates, and there are wooden chairs with gingham cushions tucked under the red table. You could call it a hotchpotch, but look more carefully and you start to appreciate how the grid of the floor is echoed by the cushions, and how the reds, greens, and blues of the wallpaper are picked up and amplified by the china and the colour blocks of the cupboards and the table. The visual impact is bold, but the design is subtle.

Gavin's sister Sasha Waddell is well known in the world of interior design, and her daughter, Atlanta Bartlett, is a stylist and author of several books on interiors. Gavin might have been even

BELOW LEFT *Colour and pattern burst into view the moment you enter the bathroom, which is wallpapered in one of the many Coles papers used in the house. As in the kitchen, Gavin has contrasted the floral prettiness with the sharp geometry of a black and white chequerboard floor. Mirrored cupboard doors give an illusion of space, and reflect a chair that Gavin has painted bright yellow and the shocking pink of the towels – a lesson in how to use colour to make the ordinary extraordinary.*

BELOW *The bathroom is a small room above the entrance hall, and would originally have been accessed from the landing. In order to make it adjoin the main bedroom, Gavin put in a second door leading directly from his bedroom, and panelled one side of it with mirror glass. The bathroom contains a shower and a lavatory, but the washbasin with its antique cast-iron stand is in the bedroom. The mustard yellow towels and emerald green cushion are the brightest spots of colour in a room of more muted, restful tones.*

OPPOSITE AND ABOVE *Gavin's bedroom, next to the turquoise drawing room, has a quieter, more English feel with its chintz curtains, sprigged and quilted bedspread, and linen-covered wing chair. The basement office is lined with books on interiors, architecture, art, furniture, fashion, and genealogy, while these bookcases are devoted to classics, including Proust whose novels he loves. Opposite the bed, the mantelpiece holds a selection of early Victorian china, reflected in a Regency overmantel.*

better known had he chosen to pursue his career as a fashion designer. In his twenties he was hailed as the next Yves St Laurent and ran his own couture company. He designed for Bellville Sassoon and his work appeared in all the fashion magazines. While still designing, Gavin started teaching and this became his vocation, first as head of fashion at Luton College, then North East London Polytechnic, and finally at Gloucestershire College. After he retired, Gavin wrote and illustrated the book *How Fashion Works*, essential reading for every serious fashion student.

Still life oil paintings by Gavin, and some of his fashion drawings, hang on the walls, and his

study is lined with books on architecture, art, interiors, furniture, fashion, and also genealogy, another subject on which he published his own book. Brought up in Scotland by an artistic mother who was widowed in the war, Gavin's talent was obvious from childhood. Sasha Waddell remembers how from the age of eight he began drawing pictures of women in long dresses, one of which she still owns. This house, too, is a work of art. Or was. Gavin has moved, the house has been sold, and its contents dispersed since these pictures were taken. It seems right that the beautiful interiors he created should live on, if only between the covers of a book.

OPPOSITE AND ABOVE RIGHT
Gavin has used wallpaper throughout the house, and in rooms where you would not expect it, such as the kitchen. All of it is from Cole & Son, which Gavin would visit with his mother and sister Sasha, buying rolls in the sale for future use. This guest bedroom is the only room where the wallpaper is not from Coles, but from Zoffany. On the mantelpiece, an early 19th-century china plate and mug, and a small abstract painting, pick up the blue of the flowers, while adding a dash of visual bite.

RIGHT *Bookshelves on either side of the chimney breast in the second guest bedroom, which is above the kitchen, are loaded with copies of* The World of Interiors, House & Garden, *and* Country Life *magazines. The fireplace is boarded over, but a Victorian needlework picture fills the blank space and the bright orange of the paper fans draws the eye to the mantelpiece.*

SELF IMAGE

THE BETTER YOU KNOW AND LIKE SOMEONE, THE
HARDER IT IS TO WRITE ABOUT THEM — THERE
IS TOO MUCH TO SAY, AND TOO MUCH BIAS. I
HAVE BEEN WORKING WITH PHOTOGRAPHER JAN
BALDWIN FOR TEN YEARS, AND BEEN A FREQUENT
GUEST OF HER AND HER HUSBAND HENRY WYNN,
WHO IS EMERITUS PROFESSOR OF STATISTICS AT
LSE AND A MAN WHOSE BREAKFAST CONVERSATION
IS MORE ENTERTAINING AND ERUDITE THAN
MOST AFTER-DINNER SPEECHES. A HOUSE BEING
ITS OWNERS' OUTER CLOTHING, I AM NEARLY AS
FOND OF THEIR REGENCY TERRACED HOME IN
CENTRAL LONDON AS I AM OF ITS OCCUPANTS.

Like its owners, this is a generous house. It doesn't have many
rooms, but it has high ceilings, a wide staircase, and a handsome
front door, painted gloss black and broad and tall enough to
convince you that it is a property of substance. It stands near
the corner of a garden square built in the 1820s, on land that
had previously been a brick and tile works. Although they vary in
size, the houses present a united front, with triangular pediments
spanning them in pairs, and twinned front doors in between.
All have a basement below pavement level and two storeys above.

OPPOSITE *In the rear half of the
ground-floor double reception room,
a Turkish kilim from Larusi sits in
front of a Robin Day leather sofa from
Habitat. Propped in the centre of the
mantelpiece, its rich colours glowing
against the background of dark grey
paint, is a fragment of early 18th-
century, embossed, painted, and
gilded Spanish leather wall covering,
restored and framed by artist
Peter Gabrielse, whose house Jan
photographed for a previous book.*

ABOVE RIGHT *The house is part of
a Regency square, set around a garden
where one of the roses is named after
the last member of the family who
owned the properties before they were
taken over by the local council or sold
in the final decades of the last century.*

RIGHT *The front window of the
double reception room has an original
shutter of an unusual sliding design,
found when the house was being
restored and now in working order.*

PAGE 76 *Looking into the entrance hall from the back sitting room past books and pictures, including framed family photographs. The small table on the left of the chair is an oak work box made for Jan when she was a child by her father, who was a cabinet maker.*

PAGE 77 *Standing in the wide entrance hall with your back to the front door, there is a view all the way through to the guest bedroom in the back extension. Stairs to the right of this room lead down to the kitchen. Hanging on the stairs to the first floor is 'Moon Baby' by Kiki Kogelnik.*

ABOVE *On a background of dark grey paint in the hall, a legacy from a shoot, hang word pictures by Alberto Duman.*

RIGHT *Above the oddly off-centre fireplace in the front sitting room hangs a series of photographs by Jan's sister Didi Baldwin. The pots are by Julian Stair. Double doors on the right open into the back sitting room.*

The estate remained in the same family until the 1980s, and although the last landlady was benign, she spent no money updating her properties. When she died and the London Borough of Islington took over as landlords, many of the houses had no bathrooms, let alone central heating. On the other hand, they had not suffered unsympathetic modernization.

Jan and Henry bought theirs in 1988. It had been empty for five years. 'We came to see it on a day when it was pouring with rain,' says Jan. 'There was something blocking the front door, and Henry and our architect James Engel were all for giving up, but I liked it and wanted to see inside. Somehow we got hold of a ladder and I climbed in through an upstairs window. There were holes in the roof and an ash tree growing up the back that was pulling off the extension, leaving a gap where a sheet of water was pouring down the wall. I managed to persuade Henry we should buy it and sold my flat in Earl's Court for exactly what we had to pay for it. I had also just bought a photographic studio in Brick Lane, so we moved in there and slept on the floor. It was pretty chaotic – with Henry's sons from his first marriage and various visiting academics staying with us on and off. I remember doing a shoot for Thomas Goode and Anatole Kaletsky picking up a coffee cup and remarking that it was rather expensive for £1.25. The label actually said £125!'

There was extensive structural work to be done: a new roof, the reconstruction of the back extension, digging down a further 45 cm/18 inches in the basement to allow for a good ceiling height, and lowering the level of the back garden so that you can step out through French doors into a paved courtyard surrounded by raised beds. The two main rooms of the basement were knocked into one to make a kitchen diner, and they installed a second bathroom with a shower in the scullery opposite the foot of the basement stairs, and transformed the front area entrance lobby and coal-hole into a utility room. The extension at entrance-hall level became the guest bedroom,

ABOVE *French doors, behind sliding shutters, open from the guest bedroom onto the higher level of the walled back garden. The bedspread is from India and the pots on the shelf above the bed are from Africa. This is the only room in the house, aside from the bathroom, that has curtains. The fabric is a piece of original Marimekko found in Portobello Market.*

OPPOSITE *Jan's office is at the same level as the kitchen in the extension, with the guest bedroom above, and the bathroom above that. It looks out onto the small, sheltered courtyard garden they dug down to create when the level of this, the lower ground floor, was lowered to give a better ceiling height.*

and above it they put in a second bathroom, using an antique roll-top bathtub found in the old scullery.

Despite its dereliction, there was a lot that could be saved: panelled doors, floorboards, plain marble chimney pieces, and a slim, almost delicate banister rail and banisters. Sealed behind old paint and wallpaper to the right of the sitting-room front window they found a recessed sliding shutter, an unusual design almost like an early pocket sliding door, that is now restored to full working order. 'We had to remortgage five times to get it all done,' says Jan, 'and it took nearly two years. My father, who was a cabinet maker, and understood about building and construction, had warned us not touch this house with a barge-pole, and in a way he was proved right. Except that we have ended up with a house that we love and couldn't possibly afford to buy now.'

ABOVE AND LEFT *The two main rooms on the lower ground floor have been knocked into one to make a kitchen and dining room. The front kitchen window looks into the area below street level, but the space feels light and bright thanks to the pale marble work surface and the graphic diagonal stripe of the Neisha Crosland fabric.*

THIS PAGE *The vintage enamel Chester gas cooker was inspired by a shoot in Germaine Greer's house.*

LEFT On a corner of the mantelpiece in the main bedroom, a framed postcard of a Victorian cyanotype photograph from the Victoria and Albert Museum is propped next to a jug of jasmine from the garden.

BELOW LEFT Hanging on the wall next to the bed are two photographs by Jan's younger sister Didi Baldwin. Jan has three siblings; all are artistic and three of them, including Jan, studied at London's Royal College of Art. Her brother Bob is a film-maker, her brother Christopher is a theatre director, and Didi is a printmaker.

BELOW When Jan and Henry bought the house there was no upstairs bathroom, but they discovered this antique roll-top bathtub in a room that would once have been a scullery, next to the kitchen at the foot of the stairs. The tub is now installed in the bathroom in the back extension between the ground and first floors. The vintage hospital trolley came from an antiques shop and the striped curtain is a piece of linen found in a French market complete with its original curtain rings.

OPPOSITE The bedroom has original fitted cupboards on either side of the chimney breast, shutters, and a view across the trees of the garden in the middle of the square. The woven bedspread is by Wallace Sewell and the poster above the bed was a present from the artist Kiki Kogelnik, a friend from Jan's time spent living in New York. The chest of drawers beneath the window was a recent find at the Criterion Auctioneers auction house in Islington, North London.

THIS PAGE AND OPPOSITE BELOW *The large landing reflects the unusual width of the entrance hall. These 'wasted' spaces help to make the house feel much bigger than its actual square footage. The glass-fronted cabinet was inherited from Henry's parents, as were the books in the oak bookcase, which were collected by Henry's mother. Looking back towards the stairs (opposite), the window above the bathroom is new, added at the suggestion of architect James Engel. This is the wall down which water was pouring when Jan first climbed in to view the house.*

The decoration and furnishings have evolved over the years. Jan has an infallible eye for line and proportion, evident in all her photographic work, and has left the architecture of the house to speak for itself; floorboards are bare, except for rugs in the living room and bedrooms, and only two windows have curtains, the rest having shutters. Most of the house is painted white. The exceptions are the fireplace wall of the back sitting room, which is charcoal grey, and the right-hand wall of the entrance hall, which is the same colour, stopping abruptly on the fourth step of the staircase where it is squared off against the white of the rest of the wall. This looks like a smart and original decorative device until Jan tells you that it was a quick paint job by her assistant Peter Dixon for a shoot some years ago.

Jan laughs that the house is 'a mess' and 'not finished'. It has never been consciously interior decorated since its first coat of white paint, and its contents are more to do with friendship, family, and travel than creating any particular impression. It's a workhorse of a house, as well as a retreat, and both Jan and Henry have offices, Jan's in the lower-ground-floor extension beneath the guest bedroom, Henry's in the back bedroom on the first floor, where he appears to have hollowed out a space for himself from a solid mass of books and papers. There are prints by Jan's sister Didi, plates by South African potter Hylton Nel, pictures by friends and colleagues, pots from trips to Africa and China, and the sewing box her father made for her.

'All my ideas are picked up from shoots,' Jan says. The kitchen is a case in point. The Rosa Aurora marble work surface was inspired by a kitchen seen on a work trip to Italy, the vintage enamel Chester cooker by a shoot in Germaine's Greer's house, and the red and white diagonal stripe of the curtains in front of the shelving was a fabric spotted when working with Neisha Crosland. 'I am lucky to see so many amazing places for work,' she says. 'In a way, it can make it more difficult to choose what to live with.'

RIGHT *The second of the first-floor bedrooms is Henry's study. Although it is lined with bookshelves, there are also books piled on the floor, stacked on the desk, and even mounded on top of the radiator. From the midst of this apparent chaos comes a stream of ideas, papers, and books relating to Henry's area of expertise, the study of mathematical statistics.*

PHOTO FINISH

You know you are in the home of people with a strong aesthetic when even the utility room is a thing of beauty. In Katie and Christopher Cornwell's house in Cheltenham, a sliding door at the foot of the stairs pulls back to reveal a wooden ironing board that slots neatly into an alcove between cupboards, it has a cover of neutral linen with a chic black stripe, and a basket on top hides the iron. The dark grey walls of the hallway contrast with the white walls of the utility room and frame this domestic vignette as if it were a spot-lit picture in a gallery.

ABOVE LEFT *Here seen from the back garden, the house dates from about 1840 and retains all its internal original features and sash windows. Christopher and Katie's refurbishment included taking out all the windows for restoration. A glazed extension on the right leads out from the dining end of the double reception room, and is where they store logs for the wood-burning stove.*

LEFT *When they first moved in, Katie and Christopher painted everything white. However, they soon realized that the rooms are sufficiently bright even on this, the lower ground floor, thanks to the size and number of*

windows, that they could introduce some drama using dark grey to make graphic contrasts, here between the white kitchen cabinets and the walls. The oven sits in the original fireplace embrasure to the left.

OPPOSITE *The kitchen floor is poured concrete and the white Formica cabinets are from Homebase. A white circular table sits on the far side of the kitchen island, and even the planting, a row of white hydrangeas, perfectly framed by the window and set against a low wall painted dark grey, reflects the interior colour scheme.*

Everywhere you look in this large, handsome early Victorian terraced house there are similar compositions, often best appreciated as views through doorways: a table in the entrance hall holding a lamp, two pottery crocks, and an unframed, misty landscape squares up with the arched opening into the inner staircase hall; walk past the stairs and look back into the sitting room and the rectangle of that doorway encloses a geometry of curves and lines created by the stripes of a rug, the splay of a Hans Wegner Peacock Chair, and the tapered legs of a side table. In the kitchen, the white Formica island is empty as virgin snow, and chopping boards and wooden spoons form a poised still life on a work surface next to the oven.

Furnishings and paintings, table lamps and ceiling lights, rugs, runners, and chopping boards, and the few, carefully chosen decorative pieces – a big antique wooden dish on the dining table, a pottery bowl on the mantelpiece, a globe atlas on a chest of drawers – all are arranged to complement one another. No clutter, nothing out of place, nothing accidental. If it were not such

OPPOSITE *On the raised ground floor at the front of the house is the sitting room. Looking into it through the door in the hall opposite the foot of the stairs, the back of a Hans Wegner Peacock Chair, which was given to them by Katie's parents, is silhouetted against one of the two tall windows, through which can be seen a second silhouette – the ironwork of an original Regency balconette. The flat-weave rug is from Roger Oates, who was Christopher's first big client. The armchair is from MADE.*

LEFT *The decoration of this elegant home everywhere serves to emphasize the crisp*

architectural detailing typical of a house of this period. Here, a cast-iron fin radiator and the striped stair runner from Roger Oates both echo the vertical stripe created by the plain, square banisters of the staircase. To the left of the mirror, a door opens onto the dining end of the double reception room.

ABOVE *At the foot of the stairs from the lower ground to the raised ground floor, a sliding door leads into the long, narrow utility room, where a wooden ironing board sits in an alcove between cupboards, perfectly framed and spot-lit like a domestic work of art.*

a comfortable house, home to three children aged 9, 15 and 19, and a Miniature Schnauzer called Fika, it might feel too controlled. Instead of which it is calm and pleasing. 'Christopher and I are both naturally tidy,' says Katie. 'When life is a bit chaotic, a sense of order is a lovely antidote.'

Tidy certainly, but also creative. Christopher is a lifestyle photographer whose clients include Center Parcs, Cathay Pacific, Nationwide, and Nespresso – work that entails frequent travel. Before the demands of three children took precedence, Katie ran her own design company specializing in paint finishes. She currently works as a teaching assistant in a local primary school. Christopher's stepfather was a television producer and director, and this is what he says sparked his love of cameras. Katie's parents have an antiques shop.

The couple met through their mothers, who are friends and live locally. At the time, Christopher's photographic studio was in the coach house of his family home, and nearby Cheltenham is where he and Katie settled when they married. After 22 years, this is their fourth home in the town. 'The first two were flats,' says Katie. 'Then we moved to a house with a garden. I would have been happy to stay, but a big Edwardian house came up for sale that gave us a lot more space. We had all kinds of plans, but when it came to the survey, we were advised not to buy it. By this time we had already moved in our heads, so we looked at other houses. This one had been on the market for a long time, and needed a lot of work, but it had all its period details, and we loved its architectural style. Fortunately, we were able to stay in our old

LEFT *The living room is L-shaped, with a seating area in the part of the room that spans the front of the house. All the period details, including the marble bullseye fireplace and the matching reeded architraves and fitted shutters, were intact, if in need of restoration and TLC. Framed over the fireplace is a piece of street art from Hong Kong and the pot on the mantelpiece is by Rina Menardi. The coffee table bench is by Hay.*

LEFT *The dining end of the living room is filled by a long antique table that holds a shallow antique wooden bowl. The room is painted in two shades of grey: the charcoal grey of the sitting end of the room, Dark Lead from Little Greene, is continued on the fireplace wall, and a lighter shade, French Grey also from Little Greene, has been used on the back wall and the wall facing the fireplace.*

house while we had it rewired and replumbed. We did very little structurally, but all the windows came out so they could be restored.'

Three years ago they moved in, and spread themselves over the three L-shaped floors, and the smaller top floor, with the two boys' rooms and bathroom at the top, two bedrooms and bathrooms on the first floor, a living room, dining room, and office on the raised ground floor, and the kitchen, utility room, playroom, and a small sitting room on the floor below. Initially it was all painted white. But they quickly realized the house was so bright, thanks to the size of the windows, that they could play with dark colours instead. Architraves, window frames, shutters, ceilings and cornices/crown moldings, cast-iron radiators, the sweeping staircase, and a few walls have remained white, as have some doors. Everything else is grey – dusky charcoal in the

kitchen, the hall, the sitting room, on one wall of the dining room, and the office, and a paler grey in the main bedroom and bathroom, and the walls of the enclosed balcony next to the dining room.

The contrasts of dark and light paintwork are graphic and crisp, and the dark walls throw anything set against them into dramatic relief, whether a framed drawing, a red light flex/cord, or the rose-pink vintage washbasin in the lavatory. Any colours that buck the monochrome trend have extra prominence. Christopher does all the brochures for Roger Oates, and it is the red stripes of the Roger Oates flat-weave rug that stand out in the living room. The grey and white stair runner, climbing from the ground floor to the top floor, is also a Roger Oates design. 'Roger is an absolute perfectionist,' says Christopher, whose house would suggest that he is almost certainly one himself.

ABOVE *At the far end of the dining room, original French doors open onto a conservatory area from where steps lead down to the back garden. The Regency glass structure has been replaced with modern glazing and the space to the right of the French doors is neatly stacked with logs for the wood-burning stove in the fireplace of the sitting room.*

OPPOSITE *Looking through the door from the staircase hall, with the sitting room through a wide opening to the left, the dining end of the room has a matching marble fireplace, its embrasure used as additional log storage. The landscape oil paintings are by Beth Fletcher and the wooden candelabra on the mantelpiece is by Design House Stockholm.*

OPPOSITE *The house extends behind the staircase. On the lower ground floor this is the kitchen. On the raised ground floor, the room directly above the kitchen is a communal home office with a block of four central desks, each with its own computer. Here the family can work together. On the day we visited, the youngest was doing homework, while Katie sitting opposite made a birthday card for a friend, and Christopher sitting next to her liaised with clients about a recent shoot. There is no fireplace, but the chimney breast is covered with cork to make a huge pinboard patterned with a changeable patchwork of family photographs.*

RIGHT *The two rooms across the front of the house on the first floor are Katie and Christopher's bedroom and this, their adjacent dressing room. Clothes hang on open rails to the left or are folded in the drawers*

of the Victorian mahogany chest of drawers that stands against a wall painted the same Dark Lead as the rooms downstairs.

BELOW LEFT *Leading off the bedroom at the back of the house, with a view of the street behind from where they access their garage, the bathroom has a wood laminate floor and a freestanding bathtub.*

BELOW RIGHT *At the foot of the bed, the television stands on a mid-century-modern rosewood sideboard. Walls are in the paler French Grey used elsewhere in the house, a quiet foil for shades of green in the khaki silk curtains, the rug, and the landscape painting by Beth Fletcher. Their daughter's bedroom and bathroom are on the same floor at the back of the house above the family office, and there are two further bedrooms and a bathroom on the top floor above.*

ART SPACE

Looking back from the first decades of the 21st century, much town planning in the years after World War II looks more like vandalism than progress. London fared better than some provincial towns, but many of its fine old houses suffered from the prevailing disregard for period architecture and lack of interest in its preservation. This square in South London dates from the late 18th century. Its wounds are no longer visible, but in the 1970s the local council converted these terraced houses into flats, knocking through party walls to make lateral conversions. While they were at it, they systematically stripped out panelled doors, fireplaces, and plaster mouldings.

ABOVE LEFT *The rear view of the house seen through the branches of a magnolia tree growing at the bottom of its garden. The conservatory extension leads out from the lower-ground-floor dining room. Replacing this with an extension with a sedum roof is next on Frank's 'to do' list for the house.*

LEFT *The kitchen, at the front of the house on the lower ground floor, has a good ceiling height and good light, thanks to being only a few steps down from street level. The reclaimed terracotta flooring replaces the* flagstones that did not survive modernization. On the left is a huge, antique cast-iron stove heater.

OPPOSITE *Where once there would have been a range, there is now a gleaming stainless steel range cooker. Frank was brought up in Holland, and the copper pans, the tiled floor, and the big earthenware bowl have a distinct flavour of the 17th-century Dutch interior about them, enhanced by the sidelong light dropping down through the area window. The tiles lined up on the mantelpiece are 17th-century Delft.*

FAR LEFT *The staircase hall is lit by the fanlight above the front door. Frank's youthful ambition was to become an architect, instead of which he read Economics and now works as a headhunter. However, his enthusiasm for architecture finds expression throughout the house, and both walls of the hall are close hung with antique engravings of buildings including Whitehall Palace by Inigo Jones, Mansion House, Eton College Chapel, and Dover Castle.*

LEFT *To the left a door opens into the raised-ground-floor double reception room, where Frank displays his collection of architectural carvings and plaster mouldings.*

More recently, the houses have been steadily reverting to private ownership, as lifelong tenants leave and the council offers them back on the open market. Frank Hollmeyer purchased his from owners who had bought from the council. Returned to its original layout of a front and a back room on each of its five floors, the house retained its sash windows, its pretty fanlight, its staircase, and some floorboards. All other internal features had gone, or had been replaced by later versions in the case of chimney pieces and skirting boards/baseboards.

Frank works as a headhunter, but outside work his interests are architecture and art. His mother is Dutch, his father German. 'I would

OPPOSITE *The two rooms on the lower ground floor have been knocked through and the room at the back is the dining room. To the right, French doors open into the conservatory extension, which Frank is planning to remodel. The antique furniture is a bold mix of styles, with painted French chairs set around a rustic pine table, in front of a glossy Biedermeier bureau.*

RIGHT *At the foot of the stairs from the hall to the dining room, a drop-leaf pine table holds an antique earthenware pot and a vase of garden flowers. Above hangs an 18th-century portrait of an unknown gentleman.*

like to have trained as an architect,' he says. 'But there were very few opportunities in Germany in the 1980s, so I took my father's advice and read Economics instead and, just for myself, I studied Flemish art of the 17th century. I was torn between the two worlds, but a friend who was a curator at the Louvre suggested I would be better off earning the money to enjoy the things I love, rather than trying to build a career around them.'

When Frank began working as an investment banker in London in the 1990s, he did just that, using his money to buy art. The only snag was that he lived in a small house in Islington, so larger purchases had to be put into storage. 'I couldn't find anywhere in Islington I could afford with the wall space I needed, so I started to look further afield. This house had lost its character, but it had high ceilings and I knew I could find a place for all my paintings.'

Frank bought the house in 2012 and moved in. 'I had plenty of ideas, but I decided to live in it for a year before changing anything.' The previous owners had used the front room of the basement as their kitchen, which is where it would always have been. A wide opening had been knocked through into the room next to it, and this was an informal living room. The raised-ground-

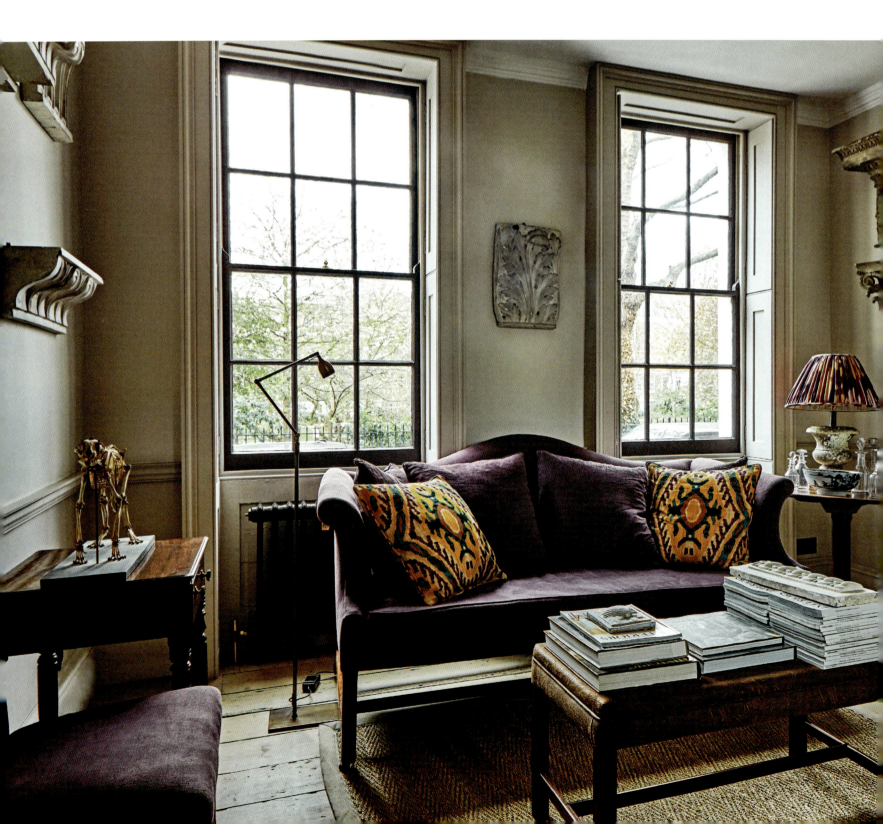

floor rooms, also linked by a wide opening, were living room and dining room, and the first, second, and attic floors were bedrooms and bathrooms.

A year of use confirmed that the kitchen should remain in the basement. The room next door to the kitchen has become the dining room, and the linked reception rooms on the floor above are living rooms. The first-floor front room, which had been the master bedroom, has become a drawing room, and the bathroom next to it Frank's study. The main bedroom and bathroom have risen to the second floor, and there are two further bedrooms in the attic.

LEFT *A pair of sash windows in the sitting room looks out on the trees of the garden at the centre of this elegant, late 18th-century square. Despite appearances, these beautifully proportioned and detailed rooms had lost all their original period features, including fireplaces, skirting boards/baseboards, shutters, and dado/chair rails. With the help of friend and architectural historian Tim Whittaker, Frank has reinstated them all. To the left of the chimney breast are two elaborate carved capitals that once graced the walls of a ballroom designed by Robert Adam. The architectural plaster casts on the left-hand wall were used to teach students of architecture.*

ABOVE RIGHT *In the rear portion of the room, a handsome 18th-century side table has legs sturdy enough to support the weight of two sizeable plaster busts, and more plaster casts hang on the wall. Walls below the dado/chair rail are painted in Farrow & Ball's Dove Tale and the old floorboards have been sanded and lightly washed with paint.*

RIGHT *Opposite the side table is a Georgian mahogany tallboy chest of drawers. The handsome 18th-century furnishings, bare floorboards, and lack of curtains combine to give these rooms a robust, masculine feel.*

It's a layout that suits the way Frank and his partner Rob Weems occupy the house. Rob works in London as co-owner and showroom manager for Solid Floor, specialists in the supply of wooden flooring, and has a house in Somerset, where the couple retreat every weekend. This is their London base, and has a more formal feel, enhanced by what an estate agent would call its 'period features', many of which are in fact 21st century. 'With the help of our friend Tim Whittaker, who is an architectural historian, we put everything back as it would have been when the house was first built in 1792,' says Frank. 'We cheated a bit in my study, where we installed a wall of panelling in an earlier 18th-century style, but in other respects, we have faithfully restored the interiors.'

The raised-ground and first-floor rooms have classical proportions, their walls horizontally divided by a skirting/baseboard and dado/chair rail and topped by a cornice/crown molding. On both floors, the space between dado and cornice has been filled with things Frank loves. In the long, narrow entrance hall hangs a tessellation of 17th- and 18th-century architectural prints. Step into the double living room and the flat planes of the architectural prints spring into three dimensions – two capitals by Robert Adam

OPPOSITE *When Frank bought the house, the rooms on the first floor were a bedroom at the front and a bathroom at the back. Frank has made the bigger of the rooms into a drawing room, and this room behind and overlooking the back garden is his study where he has 'cheated' by installing a fireplace and panelling in early 18th-century style. Walls, panelling, and all woodwork are painted Farrow & Ball's Brassica.*

RIGHT *Looking out of Frank's study, past his 18th-century painted desk to the landing, you can just see a strip of the green paint of the drawing room. The wall lamp is from a gondola, supported on a metal bracket made for it by Frank's father.*

PAGES 106–107 *The strong Calke Green by Farrow & Ball in the first-floor drawing room makes an unusual and flattering background for Frank's collection of dark 17th-century Dutch flower paintings, and portraits. The painting of a bearded gentleman was bought at auction for 'not very much money', and hangs above three 18th-century Delft peacock plates that are supported on a carved wooden capital from a church. The cushions on the sofa are made in antique Middle Eastern fabric from Susan Deliss, who also made the ikat lampshades.*

ABOVE *The two rooms on the second floor are the main bedroom at the front and the bathroom at the back. Frank credits interior decorator Scott Maddux with providing the inspiration for the bathroom, which combines patinated brass fittings with grey marble. The gilt mirror hanging above the washbasin is 18th century.*

salvaged from a demolished ballroom are hung to the left of the fireplace, a moulded acanthus leaf sprouts between the windows, and sections of cornice once used to educate students hang on the wall opposite like fragments from a particularly grandiose ruin.

In these rooms, the walls are painted in sober shades of grey, but on the floor above, the drawing room is the uncompromising green of mushy peas, and the study is lilac. Both colours make an excellent foil for Frank's paintings – 17th-century Flemish portraits and flower pieces in the drawing room, and a 15th-century religious painting in the study. Up another floor to the main bedroom, and it's back to grey, with a grisaille panel of Zuber wallpaper providing a dose of classical architecture behind the bed.

Up again, and the art on the walls on the top flight of stairs is bright and modern. Much as he loves classical architecture, Frank says that if he were ever to build a house, it would be more in the spirit of Mies van der Rohe than Palladio. Meanwhile, he is planning to replace the conservatory extension he inherited with something a bit more adventurous topped by a sedum roof. 'Not very 18th century, but there's no need to be slavish,' he says.

ABOVE AND OPPOSITE *The ceiling beams in these rooms are said to be reused timbers from ships. The flooring is new oak from Rob's company, Solid Floor. Opposite the foot of the bed Frank has hung an antique convex mirror on top of an antique Venetian mirror creating a kaleidoscope of reflections. Behind the 19th-century brass bedstead he has placed a panel of Zuber wallpaper, divided into three vertical sections as if it were a screen.*

URBAN IDYLL

TOWN OR COUNTRY? IT'S AN ENDLESS DIALECTIC. BUT WHAT IF YOU COULD HAVE THE ADVANTAGES OF BOTH — THEATRES, MUSEUMS, RESTAURANTS, AND ALL THE JOYS OF COSMOPOLITAN LIVING, PLUS FRESH AIR, 320 HECTARES/790 ACRES OF GRASSY HEATHLAND JUST DOWN THE ROAD, YOUR OWN LAWN BIG ENOUGH FOR A GAME OF BADMINTON, AND A HOUSE WITH A HALL THAT HAS SPACE FOR A REFECTORY TABLE, A DRESSER, A SIDEBOARD, ASSORTED CHAIRS, AND A GRANDFATHER CLOCK.

OPPOSITE *Set high above the city in a part of North London that was countryside, the house was built as one of a semi-detached pair by an apothecary whose shop and home had burned down in the Great Fire of London. It dates from the 1670s and despite London having spread to surround it, retains the feel of a country retreat. The kitchen would originally have been located in the basement, but has risen to occupy this large ground-floor room with its three windows looking out onto a leafy front garden, and the street beyond.*

ABOVE RIGHT *The front door was originally at the side of the house, somewhere on the wall where the grandfather clocks stands, but is now at the back such that the staircase is ahead as you enter the large dining hall. The oak dresser/hutch against the far wall holds a pair of 18th-century Chelsea porcelain 'Hans Sloane' botanical plates, and Delft.*

RIGHT *Throughout the house there are 19th-century paintings, here on a wall of the first-floor drawing room a trio of landscapes, traditionally hung on chains from a picture rail.*

PAGE 112 *At one end of the kitchen, a huge, early 19th-century oak housekeeper's cupboard with a painted arch dial clock set into its central doors (here hidden behind the open door) makes ideal storage for glasses and tableware, and other kitchen and table paraphernalia, just as it was originally designed to do.*

PAGE 113 *A sycamore dairy table makes a work surface beneath a metal ceiling rack hung with butcher's hooks from which is suspended an array of items both decorative and useful, new and old, including a leather tankard, various lanterns, and a sparkly hairband belonging to Louise.*

LEFT *The drawing room has wonderful light, thanks to windows on two sides, is hung with 19th-century oil paintings, and is full of treasures, including rare creamware mugs, early English furniture, and crewel-work pelmets. Even cushions are made from fragments of antique tapestry.*

ABOVE *On the mantelpiece, a collection of Roman glass in opalescent shades of green, blue, and gold is lined up beneath an 18th-century mirror. The smaller ones are tear bottles, used to catch the tears of mourners at funerals, and placed in the tomb as a mark of respect.*

High on a hill, overlooking the city of London and a short walk from the nearest tube station, this house, dating from the 1670s, has all the above. 'There is a story that it was built by an apothecary whose home was destroyed in the Great Fire of London,' says its owner John Stannard. 'He bought this plot when the area was a country retreat for wealthy city dwellers, and he built this house and the house next door as a pair, and lived in one of them.'

With its deep soffits and rows of sash windows set across a facade of rusty red brick, it is an undeniably handsome house, and has an unusually large footprint for London, as well as an unusually large garden. And because it is semi-detached rather than terraced, there are views from the windows in three directions.

LEFT *Hung such that it is silhouetted in the window as you enter the drawing room, and in the floor-to-ceiling side window once you are in the room, an unusual 18th-century, four-tier pewter chandelier holds beeswax candles. Thanks to the location of the house high on the hills of North London, there is a view from the window on the left over the whole of the city.*

BELOW LEFT *The 19th-century Carolean-style scroll-wing armchair in the corner of the drawing room is a recent purchase from Robert Young Antiques and looks at home against the 18th-century panelling. The paint finish, here as elsewhere in the house, is achieved with a textured paint that contains chalk dust and has the feel of original distemper.*

BELOW *The wide wooden staircase winds its way up the centre of the house with the main rooms on either side to the front and the back, and smaller rooms without windows tucked in behind it. Robert and Josyane first persuaded John and Louise that the stripped wooden banisters and dado/chair rail height panelling should be painted charcoal grey, and then convinced them that the risers should also be painted.*

OPPOSITE *On the far side of the staircase from the drawing room, this second, more informal, sitting room has windows overlooking the unusually large garden. This is the room with the television and the piano, but it also contains fine paintings and antiques, including an 18th-century oak cupboard with glazed doors, on the shelves of which are Delft and turned wooden platters, and a round pedestal side table with a wonderfully warped and undulating top.*

OPPOSITE *The master bedroom at the back of the house is dominated by a 17th-century tester bed, and hung with important Victorian paintings. There are three doors from this room, the one to the left of the chest of drawers into a bathroom, the one to the right onto the landing, and one next to the bed that opens into Louise's bathroom.*

ABOVE *John has a small study at the front of the house, next to Louise's dressing room. Modern metal shelves hold a selection of rarities and curiosities including netsuke, and a lizard in formaldehyde.*

At some point in its history, the front door, originally at the side of the house, migrated round to the back. Step through it, and it is easy to forget that you are 20 minutes from Trafalgar Square. There is a faint smell of wax polish, and the ticking of a clock. On the far wall is a fireplace and a chopping block for logs. Ahead, a wooden staircase with wide, polished treads rises up and turns before it reaches the first floor, and beyond it there is a view into the kitchen. It is an interior with the relaxed, spacious feel of a country vicarage.

John moved here from a larger 18th-century house nearby when he separated from his first wife. 'My taste has changed since then,' he says. 'That house was grander. Here, we have chosen

a quieter, perhaps less ostentatious look.' He brought little in the way of furnishings from his previous home, and his new wife, Louise, brought even less. What John did bring was a fine collection of 19th-century art, which he has been gathering since he first began his career as a lawyer some 30 years ago. There were dozens of pictures to be accommodated – watercolours, oils, drawings and prints, many of them landscapes, some of them very large, but also portraits, still lifes, and narrative paintings.

On five floors, including a basement and attic bedrooms where John's grown-up children stay when they visit, the house offers plenty of wall space. The ground and first floor each have two large rooms, one at the front, one at the back,

ABOVE *Louise's dressing room has an almost Biba-esque glamour, lined with dark fitted shelves and mirrored cupboards, and displaying her collection of vintage costume jewellery and crystals. In order to give the new joinery a feeling of age, Robert Young used what he calls 'fat' paint, which requires multiple layers of undercoat to soften the hard edges. An antique gold and black lacquered cabinet with drawers provides extra storage and the floor is painted in a bold chequerboard.*

separated by the central staircase. Behind the staircase, and between the big rooms, are smaller, windowless rooms that make ideal space for a larder and extra lavatories. Above the entrance hall and kitchen is a drawing room that runs across the front of the house, and a sitting room at the back. On the next floor are two front rooms, John's study and Louise's dressing room, and a bedroom and bathroom overlooking the back garden. Here, the in-between room is Louise's bathroom, which links her dressing room with the main bedroom.

Pictures aside, John and Louise were keen to play up the age of the house. 'It was all fitted carpet and flat emulsion,' says John. 'Which went against the architectural grain of the house. We realized we needed help to reverse this when Robert Young delivered a table we had bought from him and caught our builder about to sand the floorboards.' Robert recommended instead a gentler, if more painstaking, treatment for the old wood, using fine wire wool and elbow grease in order not to destroy its patina. And so began a partnership between Robert and Josyane, aka Rivière Interiors, and the owners. 'I already loved their taste,' says John, 'and came to trust their judgement implicitly. Occasionally we clashed, notably on the subject of the staircase. They managed to persuade me that it was a good idea to paint the banister rails and the dado/chair rail panelling in charcoal grey, but I didn't like the idea of the risers being painted the same dark colour. They won in the end, and of course they were right.'

Using paint built up in layers and mixed with added chalk, and various slightly mottled and rubbed finishes, the Youngs have created a weathered, historic finish for all the woodwork and interior walls in the house. Floorboards glow like conkers, fireplaces have been opened up, and old-fashioned fittings

OPPOSITE *On every floor there is a small, windowless room in the space behind the staircase. On the ground and first floors, one side of this space is a cupboard, the other a cloakroom with lavatory and washbasin. Here, on the second floor, it is a bathroom, and has doors linking Louise's dressing room at the front of the house with the main bedroom at the back, where John's shoes are neatly lined up under the bed. The chandelier and wall sconces hold real candles.*

ABOVE AND BELOW RIGHT *At the top of the house, on the second floor, are three bedrooms and a bathroom, used by John's grown-up children when they visit. This little room at the front has an antique brass bed and framed pages from 15th-century illuminated manuscripts hanging above it. At the foot of the bed, the wall is close hung with a collection of 19th-century prints and engravings.*

LEFT *Guests in these top bedrooms are treated to as many beautiful things to look at and admire as there are to be found elsewhere in the house. In this top-floor bedroom with its dormer windows onto the garden, there is a collection of early needlework, a late 17th-century oyster-veneered cushion frame mirror hanging above the 18th-century oak desk, and a rush light holder on the 18th-century tripod table.*

RIGHT *In a guest room on the same floor, painted a glorious sky blue, the gothic-style late Victorian brass bedstead has a Suzani bedcover. The door to the left of the fireplace opens into a bathroom in that convenient space behind the stairs. Reclining on the mantelpiece is a polychrome carving of a bearded gentleman.*

found for bathrooms. Wearing their Rivière Interiors hats, Robert takes charge of what he calls 'the hard stuff' – floors, walls, architectural detailing – while Josyane oversees fabrics and upholstery. They are both hugely knowledgeable about the early vernacular furniture and folk art that is their speciality.

Over the years, John has been advised by an impressive roster of experts, including Pre-Raphaelite specialist Christopher Newall. 'I wasn't brought up with art or antiques,' he says, 'but I grew to love them and have never been afraid to ask for help.' The contents of the house are a testament to his willingness to learn. The quality of the art on the walls, which includes works by Frederic Leighton and Holman Hunt, is matched by furnishings that date from the 18th century and back as far as the 16th century.

Thanks to comfortable sofas, plenty of rugs and cushions, and a general sense that these are rooms that are lived in and loved, the house doesn't feel like a museum, despite the fact that so many of its contents are of museum quality, whether the Roman glass on the drawing room mantelpiece, the creamware mugs on a side table, or the ivory netsuke in John's study. The quality doesn't waver. In the kitchen, an early 18th-century carved misericord supports a Greek vase, while in an attic bedroom, framed pages from a 15th-century illuminated manuscript hang over the bed. John jokingly refers to the downstairs lavatory as 'the drawing room'. It is a literal description, as the walls are hung with exquisite drawings – sketches of family members by G.F. Watts, and a self-portrait by Henry Holiday, whose painting of Dante and Beatrice first fired John's interest in art as a schoolboy.

MEMORY GAME

PLACES, PEOPLE, AND THINGS WE KNEW IN CHILDHOOD OFTEN HAVE A POWERFUL AND ENDURING INFLUENCE. EARLY VISUAL AND SENSORY MEMORIES GET RECYCLED AND REINVENTED, MAKING LINKS WITH THE PAST THAT ARE HIGHLY PERSONAL. THE INTERIOR OF THIS MID-19TH-CENTURY TERRACED HOUSE IN HACKNEY OWES AN AESTHETIC DEBT TO AN EDWARDIAN MANSION ON THE SHORES OF LOCH FYNE. THE OWNER, SOFT FURNISHINGS DESIGNER AND MAKER LUCY BATHURST, EXPLAINS THAT HER KITCHEN WAS INSPIRED BY THE TILE-CLAD WALLS AND COPPER SAUCEPANS IN THE KITCHENS OF ARDKINGLAS, AND THAT THE ROMAN BLIND IN HER LIVING ROOM, SPLASHED WITH A LARGE-SCALE PRINT OF PHEASANTS, IS THE SAME 1960 HANS TISDALL DESIGN THAT HUNG AT THE TALL WINDOWS OF ITS STUDY.

OPPOSITE *A big sofa and armchairs upholstered in velvet furnish the front part of the double reception room on the raised ground floor. Above the original early Victorian marble fireplace is propped a photograph by a friend, Barry Cawston, which Lucy has fondly nicknamed 'The Rivoli Fag Lady', as it was taken in the Rivoli Ballroom. The paint colour is Moss from Paint and Paper Library. 'I call it cowpat green and it's one of my favourite colours,' says Lucy.*

ABOVE RIGHT *At the end of the entrance hall, a window screened by a panel of antique lace looks through into the kitchen extension. The curve of the fragment of antique ironwork silhouetted in this window reflects the elegant sweep of the stair rail. The rosewood sideboard on the right is a mid-century modern piece by Danish designer Kai Winding.*

RIGHT *Coats hang beneath the turn of the staircase, where a door leads out to the side passage, and a door on the left opens onto the stairs down to the separate basement flat.*

'We had a lovely and rather old-fashioned childhood,' Lucy says. 'We lived in Hampstead, in a big house with a big garden, and every summer we all drove up to Scotland to stay with my father's best friend, John Noble, who owned Ardkinglas and was a director of the Edinburgh Tapestry Company (his son, Johnny, founded the Loch Fyne Oyster Company). While we were there, we children were left to our own devices and had a wonderful time exploring the house as well as the estate. It was my favourite place. Funnily enough, I hated that pheasant fabric when I was a child, but somehow it lodged in my brain and grew like a mushroom. When I found a length on eBay, I had to buy it. And now I love it.'

Other influences are more apparent, in particular the use of reclaimed materials, and antique and hand-crafted textiles. Coming from a line of 'terrifyingly skilled lady seamstresses', Lucy and her two sisters were taught to sew and embroider as children. At boarding school, she spent hours decorating and embellishing her room. 'I would cover the walls with magazine cuttings, and nab things from home, and everybody would come and hang out because I had made it nice.' After reading History at university, Lucy decided to concentrate on 'the things I knew I was naturally good at. I worked for a fabric company, I learned how to make curtains, did a diploma in Interior Design, and then got a job assisting Maria Speake at Retrouvius. Maria opened up a whole new world of ideas for reusing and reimagining, and in 2010 I started my own company, Nest, working with architects and interior designers making bespoke curtains and textiles for interiors, mixing old and new fabrics.'

Her time at architectural salvage and design company Retrouvius gave Lucy ample opportunity to experiment – whether using vintage army blankets trimmed with antique broderie anglaise for curtains, or making patchwork panels of old whitework and lace to provide translucent privacy at urban windows.

OPPOSITE AND BELOW *A flokati rug marks out the seating area of the reception room, while at the end that opens into the kitchen, there is a makeshift dining table, disguised by an antique linen sheet, surrounded by Kai Kristiansen chairs. The pendant lamp is from Emery & Cie and the fabric for the blind is by Hans Tisdall. On the other side of the window that looks from the entrance hall into the kitchen extension, a Regency drop-leaf table holds a vase of flowers from Scarlet & Violet.*

RIGHT *A strip of rosy copper splashback, above the slate work surface along one side of the kitchen, recalls the copper pans Lucy remembers from childhood holidays.*

PAGES 128–129 *The kitchen is new, built on top of the original basement extension. Walls are lined with reclaimed brick tiles, like the ones in the Edwardian kitchens at Ardkinglas, and all the woodwork and lighting are also reclaimed, the work surface on the right made from ironwood, once part of Brighton's West Pier, the one on the left made from billiard table slate. Steps lead down to the garden.*

BELOW *On either side of the chimney breast at the dining end of the reception room are metal lawyer's cabinets. The antique dealer was unable to open them, so they were sold at a discount. Fortunately, Lucy has a friend who is an expert locksmith. The wall lights above them are by Gaetano Sciolari.*

OPPOSITE *Hanging at the front window, and providing privacy from the street, is one of the 'Lacies' made by Lucy's company Nest from pieces of antique lace and whitework. The standard lamp, made from an antique measuring stick, is also her own design. The armchairs are covered in hand-dyed velvet by Kirsten Hecktermann and the deep sofa in hand-dyed French linen by Polly Lyster.*

She says that her stint there also taught her how 'to think like an interior designer', and her house is proof of her skills. When she bought it in 2005, the property hadn't been decorated for at least 40 years. The basement was still divided into kitchen, pantry, scullery, and larder, and had all its original fitted cupboards, and there were two reception rooms on the raised ground floor and two bedrooms and a bathroom on the floor above. Lucy decided to make the basement into a separate flat, and to build above the single-storey kitchen extension in order to have a second kitchen at raised-ground-floor level. 'I worked with architect James Stevens, and became my own client – an extremely demanding one, slightly to my surprise.'

The double reception room to the right of the staircase hall now branches at one side into a long narrow room, following the lines of the hall and projecting into the garden. Lit by skylights, two side windows, and French doors at the far end, every architectural element of this galley kitchen has a history. Walls are lined with off-white, brick-shaped tiles, nicely worn and weathered, a little bit scuffed at the edges, and very likely from an Edwardian kitchen such as the one at Ardkinglas. The wall lights once hung over bunks on a ship, illuminating bedtime reading for sailors, and the pendant Holophane lights hung in a factory. Cupboard fronts are in wood from school laboratories. On one side they are topped by billiard table slate, and on the other glossy ironwood that was once part of Brighton's West Pier. The wall opposite the window is panelled with planks of old pine, which also make shelving. Despite its age, Lucy says the wood still exudes a scent of resin when the kitchen gets hot and steamy. As for the copper pans of Ardkinglas, they are honoured with a copper sheet splashback shiny enough to make rosy reflections.

In the living room, the recycling is of the softer variety. The big window onto the street is veiled by one of Lucy's 'Lacies', and chairs and

LEFT *With the help of architect James Stevens, Lucy 're-jigged' the layout of the rooms upstairs to make a bedroom and adjoining bathroom at the back of the house, and a second bedroom and adjacent bathroom at the front. Shelves in reclaimed teak frame the doorway between her bedroom and bathroom, and the flooring is also reclaimed teak.*

BELOW LEFT *In Lucy's bathroom there is no bathtub but half the room is taken up by a walk-in shower behind a floor-to-ceiling glass screen in front of which stands the pedestal washbasin. The wall tiles are from Emery & Cie, and the red line of tiles at dado/chair rail level is picked up by a red stripe in the plain linen curtain of the window just out of view to the right.*

OPPOSITE *The same shade of coral red is echoed in cushions on the bed, and the old velvet curtains, which are a softer shade, more apricot than coral, especially at their leading edges where they have faded to a beautiful pale pink. Hanging above the bed are two oriental silk embroidered panels mounted on bookbinding fabric.*

BELOW *The bedroom at the front of the house is currently rented out to Lucy's friend Nick Hughes, an illustrator and artist, who has his own bathroom with a washbasin rather surprisingly set into a repurposed poultry incubator. One of Lucy's 'Lacies' protects his privacy covering the lower panes of the sash window. The curtains are also by Lucy and made from thick woollen army blanket, which contrasts with the bands of antique broderie anglaise and brown velvet.*

sofas are covered in antique linen and velvets hand-dyed by Kirsten Hecktermann. Upstairs, there are army blanket curtains trimmed with brown velvet and broderie anglaise at the window of the front bedroom, and in Lucy's bedroom the view of the garden is framed by a pair of second-hand velvet curtains in softest apricot pink, faded at the edges. 'I love the delicious richness of old velvet,' says Lucy. 'I am like a magpie when it comes to fabrics, and my other weakness is lighting – sparkly things like the Gaetano Sciolari wall lights in the living room.'

The garden is particularly large for London, and surrounded by the greenery of other gardens. 'I wanted outdoor space for my Collie, Finn, and so I pored over maps to find streets where there were big gaps between the backs of houses,' she says. 'This area was due to be cleared after World War II to make way for the largest housing estate in Europe. But the residents made such a fuss, the plan was shelved.' At the bottom of the garden is an open-fronted wooden summer house, built by a company called Shackadelic and clad in offcuts from the upstairs teak flooring. It's a grown-up den complete with wood-burning stove, stone sink, and deep fitted benches covered with flokati rugs and sacking cushions – a place, like Lucy's room at school, calculated to encourage loitering. 'I look round now it is all finished, and can't quite believe I am the sort of person who owns a house like this,' she says.

OPPOSITE *Lucy's Border Collie, Finn, aged 15, lies napping in the sunshine in the big open-fronted summer house at the bottom of the garden. Finn could be said to be responsible for Lucy's decision to buy this house, as her priority was to find somewhere with a large garden for him to run around in. By a quirk of planning history, the houses on this road have particularly long gardens.*

ABOVE *The summer house is designed for all-year lounging and the fitted benches are padded with cushions covered in hessian that hang from hooks in the ceiling when not in use. Flokati rugs kept in a wooden chest can be thrown over them for extra softness and there are also cushions covered in vintage sacking.*

RIGHT *Spanning the width of the garden, the summer house also has space for a small wood-burning stove, and a kitchen area on the left with a stone sink. It was built by a company called Shackadelic.*

BUILDING ON THE PAST

IN HIS DIARY OF 1994, THE ARCHITECTURAL HISTORIAN AND SHARP SOCIAL OBSERVER JAMES LEES-MILNE RECORDED LUNCH AT THE HOME OF RORY YOUNG, WHOM HE DESCRIBED AS 'A RADIANT YOUNG CRAFTSMAN, FULL OF ENTHUSIASM, LEARNING, EXPERIENCE OF OLD BUILDINGS'. SUMMING UP RORY'S HOME, HE SAID: 'NICE ARTISAN HOUSE ... WHICH HE HAS JOLLIED UP AND MADE EXTREMELY ATTRACTIVE.'

Nearly a quarter of a century later, the only word of this that seems inappropriate is 'young', although Rory continues to live up to his surname; now in his mid-sixties, he is able to lift a stone slab without any apparent difficulty. His enthusiasm remains, while learning and experience have grown, as has his reputation in the world of building conservation and restoration. Rory has also gained recognition as a sculptor – though he prefers the anonymity of 'niche filler'. Among his commissions since James Lees-Milne's visit are the carving of 16 scenes from Genesis for the Great West Door of York Minster, and seven statues of martyrs for the nave of St Albans Cathedral.

ABOVE LEFT *Rory's principles in his conservation restoration of this relatively humble terraced townhouse were to 'honour the building while adding layers of interest and beauty'. In the entrance hall, his additions have included a marbled chimney piece and flooring in new flagstones.*

LEFT *From the entrance hall, there is a view past the stairs to the kitchen, where doors open onto the courtyard garden. The glazed partition on the left was created from an old door. Both the grandfather clock and the*

chair were inherited with the house, which Rory bought complete with sitting tenant, an old lady who had worked as a cleaner at his auctioneer grandfather's office.

OPPOSITE *In the kitchen Rory built a handsome chimney piece, its design inspired by early Renaissance masonry, with intarsia in polished red silt stone, 'the poor man's porphyry'. Ranked according to size on the high mantelshelf is a wonderful swoop of Victorian pottery, including a collection of mochaware mugs.*

The son of a Cotswold farmer, Rory discovered hands-on building when repairing dry stone walls. After art school, he set off in a Fiat van for a painting tour of England. It became an architectural tour, and the inspiration for a life devoted to the practise and history of traditional building techniques. Rory managed to find work reconstructing a 17th-century gazebo, and set about teaching himself stonemasonry, mortared walling, paving, and plastering. He became an expert in lime, which he calls 'the lifeblood of all traditional buildings' – a material that can be used as render, mortar, plaster, or paint, and has the advantage over cement of being protective, nourishing even, to the stone it coats, and also permeable, allowing a building to 'breathe'. Forty years ago, it was largely forgotten and certainly underused. Rory has been one of its most effective champions, such that today its properties and advantages are widely recognized.

The Cirencester townhouse that Rory used every penny he owned to buy at a knock-down price in 1980, and then had to spend seven years saving up to restore, and four years to finish, has become a place of pilgrimage for anyone interested in historic buildings, their construction, and preservation. In his courtyard garden, there is a lime pit for demonstrations, and every so often he gives illustrated talks on aspects of his work, rearranging his drawing room to seat an audience of as many as 29. Which sounds ambitious, until he tells you that he had a party before Christmas for 94.

This is not a big house, nor does it have any particular architectural distinction. Three-storey, flat-fronted, its door opening directly onto the

LEFT *The kitchen table, also Rory's desk, is laid for lunch with turned wooden plates made by Judith Verity. Woodwork and panelling are painted a soft green, subtly stippled by craftsman-painter Mike Reynolds. The 18th-century Chinese export blue and white platters on the far shelf were found, still hanging on the wall but bizarrely covered by old wallpaper, in Rory's mother's great-grandparents' house. The glazed door opens into the scullery.*

pavement, the front half dates from about 1820 and the rear from 1850. On this street of pretty terraced houses near the market square, it is like the governess at the ball – quiet, plain, simply dressed. Rory was living next door in a property owned by his parents when the house came up for sale and, blighted by a disastrous trio of sitting tenant, damp, and subsidence, failed to sell. But Rory liked it, and not just because it was cheap. 'It had a poignant atmosphere,' he says. 'I wanted to coax it back to life.' Like the vernacular builders of the past that he so admires, he had very little money, but plenty of time and know-how.

His restoration was thorough, sensitive, and impressively economical. Every scrap of the original fabric, whether stone, brick, or timber, was saved and reused. Even the crumblings of old lime mortar were crushed, sieved, and refreshed with new lime putty. As the work progressed, Rory added his own embellishments: a fireplace in the kitchen inlaid with lozenges of polished red silt stone, a faux panelled door carved in limestone in the side passage from the street to the backyard, blocking a redundant entrance,

BELOW RIGHT *In the outhouse workshop adjoining the scullery, jam jars of coloured limewash are stacked on shelves and labelled according to where they have been used.*

OPPOSITE *The outhouse furthest from the house and accessed from the courtyard is the old wash house and*

retains its fireplace and chimney. Restoring this building for use as an on-site workshop was one of Rory's first projects, achieved with the help of craftsman-builder Ian Constantinides. Most of Rory's sculptural commissions are for churches and have included seven painted statues of martyrs for St Albans Cathedral.

ABOVE *Looking into the scullery from one of the workshops that run along one side of the courtyard garden. The kitchen is to the right, and there is a larder with slate shelves through the green door ahead. The huge glazed sink was rescued by Rory when he was told that the owners of the farmhouse where he was brought up were throwing it out. He has mounted it on a pair of fluted brackets. Set into the window embrasure is a stone plaque carved with words by William Morris.*

RIGHT *Glazed double doors from the kitchen open into the courtyard garden, in which there is a well, and a lime pit for slaking lime.*

and a completely new room constructed over this passage using reclaimed stone. Friends and partners contributed. Artist Jane Rickards frescoed the interior of the room above the passageway, and Ursula Falconer added gilded stars to its ceiling; Judith Verity turned the wooden handles for the kitchen cupboards; James Witchell made the brilliant-cut glass for some of the windows; Ian Constantinides, who later formed St Blaise Builders, helped him to rebuild the outside shed, once a wash house, to make a workshop.

A mark of this craftsmanship is how well the house has matured. Rory's additions, whether the smooth expanse of flagstones and carved chimney piece in the entrance hall, the salvaged door with original bottle glass that acts as a partition between the kitchen and the stairs, or the stone sink rescued from the farmhouse where Rory spent his childhood when he was tipped off that it was being thrown out, and which now rests on a pair of fluted brackets, have all settled into place. Paint colours inspired by historic interiors and the palettes of painters, including Degas and Giotto, make a rich background for pictures and furnishings, including a few fine antiques inherited from his parents, and paintings by his mother, who was an artist. The grandfather clock and 18th-century country carver chair in the kitchen both came with the house.

Everything in these comfortable, layered, lived-in rooms has a highly personal meaning for Rory. Lunch is served on beautiful turned wooden plates made by his ex-partner Judith Verity, while

OPPOSITE *The drawing room is on the first floor spanning the front of the house and, as befits its status, is the only room with wallpaper, a Cole & Son design that Rory 'fell in love with' and bought several rolls of in 1983 because it was being discontinued. He was not able to use it on these walls until 1991. The room is often the venue for parties and also for talks on conservation and vernacular building, its materials and techniques. The rag rug in front of the fireplace was made by Rory's mother Jill Young, who was an artist.*

RIGHT *Rory studied painting at Camberwell School of Arts and Crafts. One of his paintings, an atmospheric interior in collector Warner Dailey's house, hangs in the drawing room above an early 19th-century sideboard, and there is a self-portrait on the landing. Despite his evident talent, he was not encouraged, and turned his attention to vernacular architecture. On the other side of the landing, just glimpsed through the open door, is a bathroom, and next to it, a bedroom.*

OPPOSITE *A door from the main bedroom on the first floor leads into the small chamber Rory calls the 'oratory', a completely new room that he built with a facade of reworked stones above the side passage from the street to the rear courtyard – 'an aedicule (small shrine), in the Cotswold late 17th-century vernacular', its walls decorated with fresco, its ceiling with gilded stars. Cupboard bookshelves with panelled doors fill the alcove to the left of the fireplace and the patchwork quilt was made by Judith Verity.*

LEFT *The window opposite the bed is shrouded with the draped greenery of pot plants and there are more books on shelves to its right and in the glazed cabinet book shelf sitting on top of the chest of drawers.*

PAGE 146 *The second-floor bedroom is above the drawing room and also has two windows onto the street. To the left of the left-hand window, this pretty set of Regency painted shelves hanging above a chest of drawers holds some of the early china that Rory loves and collects, including a New Hall 'slop bowl' second from the right on the top shelf, from a late 18th-century tea set, used for holding the dregs of cold tea. Flowers throughout the house are by Rory's friend Pauline Travallion.*

PAGE 147 *At the foot of the antique metal bed in the same bedroom, a bowl of homemade rose petal potpourri stands on a 17th-century English oak table. The oil painting of a garden to the left of the bed is by Anne-Catherine Phillips, a painter friend from Rory's Camberwell student days. Above this room is an attic space where Rory stores plaster maquettes for some of his sculptures.*

coffee comes in cups by potter and friend David Garland. The rag rug in front of the drawing room fireplace was made by his mother, who also bought the armoire at the other end of the room, which had belonged to the artist Frank Cadogan Cowper. A small marble sarcophagus on the landing was left to Rory by James Lees-Milne. Many of these connections are explained in notes, written by Rory and pinned behind a door, or inside a drawer, or on the back of a picture.

Words as well as images are important in this house. The kitchen panelling is covered with a mosaic of postcards – written by friends and sent to this address – while the table is piled with papers, and there are books in almost every room, lined up on bookshelves, or stacked on tables. An old school slate hanging in the kitchen is engraved with the names and dates of birth of Rory's seven godchildren. On the stairs, stone plaques engraved by Rory, who is regularly commissioned to design and carve headstones, pronounce 'May the blessing of light be on you, light without and light within' and, beside the door of his workshop, 'Entertain strangers and encounter angels unawares'. In the rebate of the scullery window are the famous words by William Morris 'Have nothing in your house that you do not know to be useful or believe to be beautiful'.

OPPOSITE *In the second-floor bedroom at the back of the house, an antique patchwork quilt made from triangles of early 19th-century sprigged, checked, and striped cottons covers the bed. Roman pottery bought by Rory's grandfather is arranged on the mantelpiece, beneath an oil painting by his mother Jill Young.*

ABOVE *Pinned to the back of the door from the landing to the same bedroom is a postcard of a painting by Degas using a very similar colour palette to the green and shades of terracotta of the walls and woodwork. Rory used inspiration from a variety of sources, including works of art, and nature – 'for instance from auriculas and licheny rocks' – for the decoration of the house, aiming for 'a lambent and elevating atmosphere that I would be happy to live with'. On a blocked-in door to the adjacent*

bathroom hangs a painting in the manner of a 17th-century Dutch flower piece, also by Jill Young.

ABOVE RIGHT *Banisters are painted dark slate grey and the walls of the staircase are a rich, Pompeian red, an ideal background for framed architectural engravings. The slate plaque on the left, with engraved and coloured lettering, is by Rory, who is often asked to design and carve memorial stones and headstones.*

RIGHT *Next to the bedroom is a second bathroom painted blue and cream. From the window, you can see across to a house that once belonged to his aunt and uncle and that he bought from his cousins, the garden of which will allow him to expand his own garden and create a nymphaeum.*

CONTEMPORARY CRAFT

When, in 1967, architect Peter Moiret planned a development of terraced houses in South London, built on land that was once the garden of an 18th-century house, his aim was to attract families and create a sense of community. The footprint of each house is small, but they are set around a generous area of grass and trees, which is open and more like a village green than the railed gardens of older London squares. The ground floor was designed to incorporate a single garage, the first floor is an open-plan living room, and there are three bedrooms and a bathroom on the top floor. Every house has a balcony, either at the front or the back, placed in order to catch the best of the sun. For the same reason, the kitchens were originally located either on the ground floor at the back or on the first floor.

OPPOSITE *The ground floor has been opened up to make a single kitchen and dining room such that the original 1960s open-tread staircase can now be seen from all angles, and is not boxed in by partition walls as it originally would have been. One of the earliest residents of the estate has described seeing the pine newel posts for all the houses on the estate arriving from Scandinavia on a lorry.*

ABOVE RIGHT *Looking from the back of the garden across Charlene's lush planting to the rear of the house. The ground-floor glass sliding doors are new, but the windows above were restored rather than replaced.*

RIGHT *The change in ceiling level of the ground floor marks the original dividing wall between the lower-ceilinged garage and the old kitchen and dining room.*

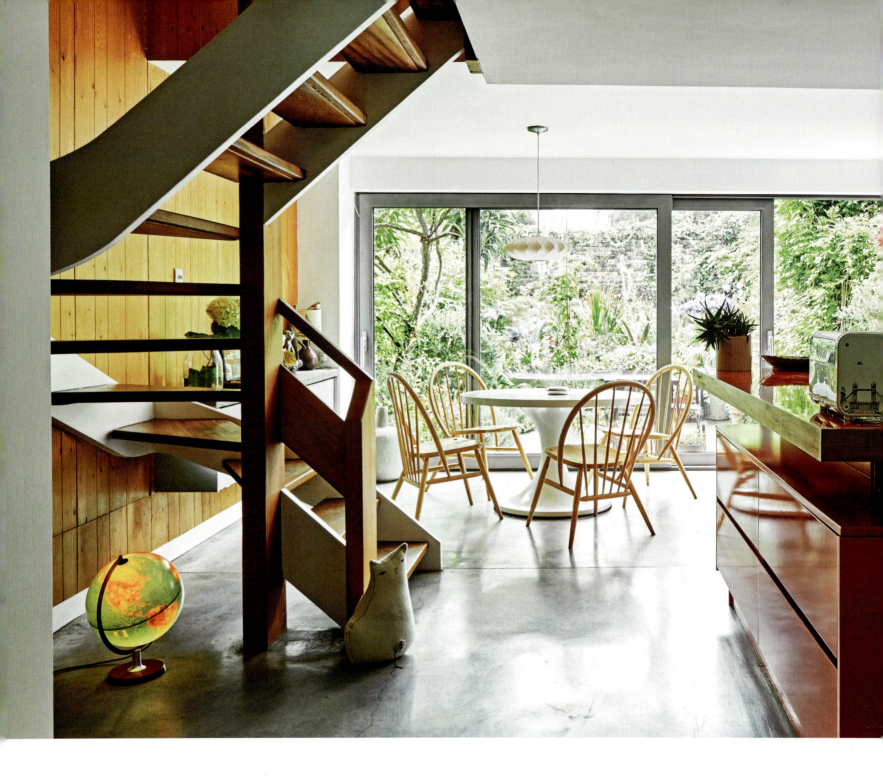

Half a century on, and these houses are desirable as ever, a few still occupied by people who moved in when they were brand new. Textile and home accessories designer Charlene Mullen bought hers 11 years ago. 'There really is a sense of community,' she says. 'I have good friends who are neighbours, and it's great for children – they all play in each other's gardens.' These are things she has come to appreciate, but her initial reason for buying was more aesthetic than social. 'I wanted somewhere modern,' she says. 'I had been living in Peckham, and felt I had done the Victorian thing. I wanted a project, a fresh start. I made an offer on this straight after I viewed it.'

At the time Charlene was working as a freelance textile designer in fashion, selling her prints and embroidery designs to everyone from River Island to Donna Karan. 'I had quite a tight budget to do this place up. I worked with Dive Architects (now based in Sweden). The ground floor was still a garage, there was a downstairs lavatory off the hall, and a small kitchen and dining room across the back, opening onto the garden. We took out the internal walls in order to make one big space, keeping a separate lavatory. At the same time we restored or replaced all the windows and updated the heating.' To help keep the heat in, the flat roof was given an extra layer of insulation.

LEFT *As you come through the front door you are greeted by a wide-screen view through sliding glass doors of the garden, the back wall of which once sheltered the vegetable garden of a large Georgian house. The floor is polished concrete and helps to reflect light into the front part of the room, which was the garage and where there are no windows. The Dualit toaster is decorated with Charlene's London skyline design.*

RIGHT *The garden is densely planted, and full of plants in big pots. Smaller pots have migrated indoors, here to the end of the run of fitted kitchen cupboards nearest the doors to the garden. The carcass of the kitchen was made in MDF, which has been sprayed a grey-green. The work surface is Polyrey. Charlene bought the plate, which is Dutch, as a reward for herself 'for surviving Maison et Objet', the big Paris trade show.*

BELOW RIGHT *Wallpaper from Linda Florence in the downstairs cloakroom reflects the kitchen colour scheme of red and green.*

Charlene and her cat camped in a room upstairs while the work progressed. 'It wasn't comfortable, but the advantage was that I could project manage, and help keep costs down. For example, when the architects specified doors for the kitchen, I was able to find the same thing online for a lower price. They persuaded me not to go for a white kitchen, so instead I chose red and a sort of grey-green, and I haven't got bored with it yet. We used MDF for the carcass and the work surfaces are Polyrey.'

From the outside, the house looks much as it always did, complete with metal up-and-over garage door. The residents' association ensures that the exteriors remain uniform, so the

garage door is painted dark green, just like all the others. At first- and second-floor levels there is weatherboarding, and this is painted white. Because you assume there is a garage, when the front door opens onto an expanse of polished concrete flooring, the sense of spaciousness is surprising, and the wide wall-to-wall view straight through to the garden unexpected. Perfectly framed by the long oblong of sliding glass doors, the sunlit foliage is bright as a cinema screen. To the left an open-tread wooden staircase takes a turn towards the first floor, to the right a long kitchen island is clad in glossy poppy red, and ahead four Ercol chairs arch their bentwood backs around a white, circular table. Simple ingredients for an arresting effect.

Soon after the house was finished, Charlene changed direction and started a business under her own name, applying her delicate, confident line drawings to interiors rather than clothing.

ABOVE *Charlene creates new designs on her sewing machine, set on a long trestle table from the London offices of Dive Architects, who helped her with the house, and who subsequently moved their practice to Sweden. A door opens onto the balcony that runs along the front of the house, overlooking the mature trees of the communal garden at the centre of the estate. Behind her hangs one of her 'Sampler' lace panels.*

LEFT *Suspended from the ceiling at one end of the oversized work table is a ceramic mobile by friend and artist Daniel Reynolds.*

OPPOSITE *At the far end of the same window is one of Charlene's embroidered panels, which are handmade for her in India, its leaves echoed by the elephant's ear begonia on the sideboard in front.*

THIS PAGE *A Matthew Hilton sofa fills the corner of the higher level of the first-floor living room, decorated by a selection of Charlene's hand-embroidered cushions, and a hand-embroidered throw that is laid along its back. It was too big to come up the stairs, so was brought in through the front windows instead. The rug is also by Charlene, the folded blanket is by Eleanor Pritchard, and the coffee table is by Bethan Gray.*

THIS PAGE *On an original fitted shelf in the front half of the living room, running along the section of wall behind which is the staircase, an arrangement of favourite pieces is watched over by a pair of African funeral masks. The china dog and cat are by Susan Parkinson, and the striped pots are from Rye Pottery. Flowers are from the garden. The yellow paint chart with pastiche colour titles is an artwork by Wil Roberts.*

Scanned, digitized, and hand-embroidered in India to make cushions, lampshades, and fabric panels, her designs were instantly popular – the etched London skylines, complete with skyscrapers, a helicopter, and Tower Bridge, are particularly distinctive. She was commissioned by Royal Doulton, and by Dualit, and more recently has added to her portfolio with cotton lace panels woven in Glasgow, and rugs, made to commission and hand-knotted in Nepal.

The bright upstairs living room, which has a wall of windows at the front and the back, is an ideal showcase for Charlene's work. It is also the place where her ideas begin, at a sewing machine on a long trestle table, where she sits with her back to the balcony and its view of the communal gardens.

RIGHT *The pleasing geometry of the staircase, with its pine newel post and banisters and hardwood treads, has a strong presence on the ground and first floors, rising up to a small landing on the second floor.*

Behind her, and shading her from an excess of sunlight as she works, hangs one of her lace panels, scattered with images from inspirations as diverse as 18th-century cutwork, a glimpsed tattoo, early graffiti, a 17th-century woodcut, and scientific diagrams.

The room is on two levels, and on the raised level overlooking the garden there is a Matthew Hilton corner sofa, with a heavily embroidered length of linen along its back, and a scattering of embroidered cushions in simple, geometric patterns, all by Charlene. Framed embroideries inspired by scrimshaw, among other things, hang along the wall, and the Bethan Gray coffee table stands on one of her 'Tear Drop' rugs. Beside the sofa, an embroidered lampshade tops a chunky turned wooden lamp base by De La Espada. Other pieces are by artist friends such as Daniel Reynolds, who made the ceramic mobile that hangs at one end of her work table, and by artist-makers whose work she admires, including a ceramic dog and a cat by Susan Parkinson, and a striped vase from Rye Pottery. On the top floor, the wall lights above her bed are her own design, as are the cushions on the Ercol armchair, and the rug.

In a house with a flat roof, no basement, and little wasted space, storage is not plentiful, especially now the garage has been swallowed up by the kitchen. Charlene currently shares the house with a lodger who is studying lighting design, and uses the third bedroom as a substitute attic. 'I got side-tracked when I opened the shop in 2013,' she says. 'There are still so many things I would like to do with this house – new flooring in the living room, more cupboards. But I will definitely stay. It's a lovely place to live.'

OPPOSITE *Like the living room below, Charlene's bedroom at the front of the house is a private showcase and testing ground for her own designs. The rug was hand-knotted in Nepal using a company that is part of Goodweave, an organization that aims to stop child labour in the carpet industry. The design includes a single red star, just seen under the chair. Also by Charlene are the hand-embroidered cushions and wall lamp. The bed is Hans Wegner and was bought online, and the picture is an embroidered collage dating from the 1970s.*

ABOVE RIGHT *In a corner of the bathroom, a succulent with little round leaves, so perfectly spaced it hardly looks real, dangles in a macramé pot holder from O'Dell's Studios. The fringed towels are from Jaipur, and the blind is in one of Charlene's block prints.*

RIGHT *The second floor is the only part of the house that is not open plan. Here there are two rooms at the back, a bathroom and bedroom, and two bedrooms at the front, one of which Charlene is currently using as storage space.*

SEASIDE INSPIRATION

MELANIE MOLESWORTH SAYS THAT SHE HAS ALWAYS BEEN 'A NATURE GIRL. AS A CHILD I COLLECTED BUTTERFLIES. I HATCHED SILKWORMS IN THE AIRING CUPBOARD, AND I HAD A VIVARIUM WITH SLOW WORMS. AFTER SCHOOL I HAD NO IDEA WHAT I WANTED TO DO — PROBABLY SOMETHING ARTY — BUT I DEFINITELY DIDN'T WANT TO STAY AT HOME. SO I WENT TO LONDON AND GOT A JOB AS A SECRETARY AT HARVEY NICHOLS.' FROM WHERE, AFTER A SHORT HOP VIA THE ADVERTISING DEPARTMENT OF *HOUSE & GARDEN* MAGAZINE, AND A SKIP TO PA TO THE EDITOR OF *BRIDES*, MELANIE MADE THE JUMP INTO EDITORIAL AND WORKED IN FASHION BEFORE SETTLING ON INTERIORS AND BECOMING HOME EDITOR.

ABOVE LEFT *A new staircase, leading from one of the two front doors, arrives at a small landing where this door with its glazed surround opens into the huge 18-metre/60-foot living room and kitchen, a space that had been used as assembly rooms, and then by the Lyme Regis Conservative Club, before it became an artist's studio. Framed in a glass-fronted cabinet on the wall are fragments of china and pottery found by Melanie on the beach.*

LEFT *At the kitchen end of the room, there is a single arched window in the* end wall, but at this, the sitting end, there are also windows on both sides, here looking out onto the courtyard garden at first-floor level, which is reached across a metal bridge. The round table holds a selection of stripy vases and to its left is the frame holding the sheets of Victorian pressed seaweed that inspired Melanie's new business with fellow stylist Julia Bird.*

OPPOSITE *The kitchen table was bought from Bridport Market and sits on a rectangle of floor painted in a large chequerboard using Farrow & Ball Hague Blue and White Tie.*

Since then, as a freelance stylist, Melanie has worked on many magazines, written a best-selling book, *Junk Style*, and styled for Marks & Spencer, Laura Ashley, and The White Company, among others. For 15 years, she and her husband Martin Dennis, a TV director, and their two sons lived in Chiswick. About ten years ago they started to consider moving out of London – 'The boys were leaving home, and I had always hankered after the countryside,' she says. With her father in Dorset, and other family and friends in the South Hams, they looked in the West Country, with the idea of finding somewhere small, and buying a flat as a London base.

'We saw the particulars for this house a long time before we decided to view it,' says Melanie. 'It had been hanging around for ages, was more than we wanted to spend, and enormous. A friend who loved Lyme Regis persuaded us that we should look at it, and when we did, it was obvious it had potential. We asked another friend, architect Ed Howell, for ideas and he came up with a plan for dividing it so that we could have a rental property, and an income.' They took the plunge, sold their house, ditched the idea of a London flat, and moved in. 'It was 2011, and I was very hot and cold about it, very nervous. But actually, it's been amazing.'

OPPOSITE *Melanie and Martin inherited a fitted kitchen that was already in place, but have given it a facelift by painting it Farrow & Ball Mole's Breath and replacing the handles. New white brick tiling, open shelving, and a wall-mounted metal saucepan rack completed the transformation. A sofa covered in navy blue linen, just seen to the left, marks the division between the kitchen and the sitting room.*

RIGHT *To the left of the big, arched window that lights the kitchen, a table holds a framed pressed seaweed by Molesworth & Bird propped against an old seed tray, another find from Bridport Market. To its right is a painted Swedish sofa. A broken piece of brick, deliberately placed, takes on the status of a small sculpture. Lou-Lou the cat watches proceedings from under the table.*

ABOVE *Hanging across the door to the garden, between the kitchen and sitting room, is a dip-dyed linen curtain from Designers Guild. To the left of it, the top of an old plan chest houses a selection of plants, pottery, and bowls holding a fascinating and beautiful collection of objets trouvés including feathers, pebbles, a bird's skull, a butterfly wing, dead beetles, and a bent and rusting fork.*

LEFT *Behind the sofa that faces the kitchen table, more of Melanie's finds are on display, here shells and fossils from local beaches. Next to them, not seen, is a glass tabletop cabinet, made by Martin, who has a woodworking workshop on the floor below, and holding a selection of bent and battered cutlery, all also found on the beach. Melanie cites Kettle's Yard as having long been an inspiration.*

They have certainly found an amazing place to live – down a side road, but only yards from the seafront, in one of Dorset's prettiest seaside towns. From the outside the house is ordinary, terraced and with a plain facade of two doors with fanlights, and five sash windows, two at street level, three above. The door to the left leads into The Arched House, their five-bedroom rental property, which Melanie has furnished and decorated with characteristic style. The door on the right, however, takes you up a flight of stairs to something completely unexpected.

THIS PAGE *The deep ledge that runs at chest level around the whole room was already in place and is a favourite feature – 'So great for not having to make final decisions,' says Melanie, who often adds, takes away, or moves its contents, here a painting of aubergines by Lucy Dickinson and some vintage doll's-house furniture, among other things.*

On the first floor, at the back, the house balloons from urban terrace into a vast single space a good 18 metres/60 feet long, with the kitchen at one end and the living room at the other. 'Our whole London house would have fitted into this room,' says Melanie, 'and we have a big storage room and Martin's workshop below, a bedroom and bathroom at this level, and three more bedrooms and a bathroom above.' Bedrooms belonging to the rental property interlock with Melanie and Martin's part of the house, making it impossible to visualize without a floor plan. 'When we bought it, the layout was even more confusing,' says Melanie, 'and you could only access our part of the house from a staircase in The Arched House. Ed made it work by putting in the second staircase.'

No one knows what the big room was originally used for. There is a photograph from the beginning of the last century showing it hung with bunting and crammed with long trestle tables for a celebratory meal. More recently, it was the Conservative Club, and

The huge sofa, big enough to seat six, came with the house, and has been re-covered in a dark grey linen. A white IKEA table stands between two armchairs, one covered in a floral fabric by Paul Smith for Mulberry. The window overlooks the culvert for the River Lym, which runs beneath part of the house.

THIS PAGE *Mirroring the window at the kitchen end of the room, this window looks across roofs towards the sea, which is a short walk from the front door. More pressed seaweed is propped on the shelves, joined on the left by a row of cuttlefish skeletons.*

fitted with a bar and padded banquettes. The rest was a guest house, so bedrooms had been partitioned to make bathrooms, and there was a makeshift gym and a sauna in the basement. While Ed oversaw the architectural untangling, Melanie and Martin lived in one room. 'Fortunately, we had a fantastic local builder, Guy Bamford, and the whole thing only took five months.' Including painting everything white or pale grey, after which it was a question of furnishing. 'Our London stuff just disappeared in such a big space, but we inherited a huge sofa with the house, and we bought the kitchen table in Bridport antiques market. There was already a kitchen at one end of the big room, and we painted it grey, and changed the handles and the tiling. We left the floorboards as they were, though I painted an oblong chequerboard in dark blue and white where the kitchen table stands.'

Beachcombing has proved a rich decorative seam – there are cuttlefish skeletons lined up on the dado-height shelf that runs round the big room, feathers, a speckled bird's egg, and shiny beetles laid out on earthenware plates, sea glass and fragments of china in bowls, dried seed heads in jugs, and bits of rusting metal propped like small sculptures. 'I am a natural scavenger,' says Melanie, who has the alchemic knack of turning someone else's rubbish into something of beauty, whether a rusting water tank used as a side table, or a collection of bent and twisted cutlery arranged like archaeological treasures in a glass-topped cabinet.

Before they moved, or even thought of moving, Melanie had bought twelve 19th-century sheets of pressed seaweed, which she framed as a group. All are labelled and, by coincidence, all were collected on beaches in Lyme Bay. Melanie has since set up a business with friend and fellow stylist Julia Bird, who lives in Cornwall, collecting varieties of seaweed, and making their own pressings for calendars, postcards, and limited-edition prints. Scavenging at its most creative.

LEFT *Also on the plan chest next to the door to the courtyard is a BAFTA award won by Martin, a director and production manager who has worked on television comedy series including* Black Books, Men Behaving Badly, *and* Friday Night Dinner. *The dead beetles on the pottery plate were found in the house, already desiccated.*

ABOVE *Melanie bought the old envelope addressed in elegant, old-fashioned script to 'The Lady Molesworth' on eBay for £3 and framed it because it makes her laugh.*

OPPOSITE *Melanie turned her talent for creating beauty from junk into a best-selling book called* Junk Style *and has now turned her talent for foraging into an art, pressing seaweed found on local beaches. She works in a room that leads off the kitchen, and doubles as a guest room, using this press made for her by Martin. In partnership with Julia Bird, who collects seaweed from beaches where she lives in Cornwall, they make calendars, postcards, and limited-edition prints.*

OPPOSITE *The main bedroom is one of the rooms directly above the River Lym, which runs in a deep culvert down through the town and into the sea. The Victorian chair is covered in vintage William Morris fabric, and the table beneath the window has one set of legs propped on blocks of wood to compensate for the slope of the old floorboards. Also visible from this window is the pitched roof of the kitchen and living room, which run along the opposite side of the culvert from the street.*

ABOVE *Framed family photographs hang on the landing, where the new staircase from the front door leads up to the kitchen, from where a further flight of stairs leads up again to three bedrooms and a bathroom. The two adjacent houses, one lived in by Martin and Melanie, the other rented out by them for holiday*

lets, interlock with one another such that the locked door from this landing leads into one of the five bedrooms of the rental property.

ABOVE RIGHT *Melanie uses one of the three bedrooms as a sewing room, and makes all her own clothes here. Hanging from the pegs on the wall is a selection of vintage clothing, including a silk harlequin jacket from Willow Hilson in Exeter. A sleeping Lou-Lou is perfectly colour co-ordinated, as befits a stylist's cat.*

RIGHT *This bathroom, next to the main bedroom, borrows light through an internal window above the mirror. Melanie's swimming costume, from a morning dip in the sea, hangs over the side of the bathtub.*

Floral Confection

Before the industrial revolution, most people worked where they lived. Today it is less usual, but if you own a shop as pretty as that of textile designer and botanical artist Carol Lake, you might well be tempted to take up residence, which is just what she and her partner John Kitson have done. On a quiet street a short walk from the centre of Norwich, the shop where she sells her designs stands out for the glamour of its late-Victorian frontage, complete with glossy tiling, curved plate glass, and gold-on-black glass lettering. Inside, it retains its original fittings — mirror-backed mahogany shelving, and a green verre églomisé frieze with more gold lettering announcing 'chocolates ... pastilles, and clear gum ... by royal appointment'.

OPPOSITE *The original fittings and decor of this Victorian confectionery, have all survived, including the textured Anaglypta paper on the ceiling, and the verre églomisé frieze with its gold lettering. A tailor's dummy is draped with one of Carol's silk scarves, and her cushions fill the lower shelves. The shop also stocks scented candles by Cire Trudon, a selection of which sits under glass domes on the marble shelf with its mirrored backing.*

ABOVE RIGHT *On a side street, a five-minute walk from the historic centre of the city, Carol's shop sits in a row of independent retailers, with an artisan bakery to its left and a shop specializing in antique bathroom fittings on its right. The shop front is also original.*

RIGHT *Looking through to the back room of the shop where a glazed partition separates the old building from the new extension – a big, bright kitchen and living room, at one end of which Carol has her studio.*

The shop is open on Saturdays, or by appointment (not royal). At other times you can peer through the window to see Carol's vibrant floral cushions stacked on the shelves, silk scarves draped around the necks of vintage mannequins, and right through the shop to the bright space beyond, which is Carol's studio and also her kitchen. At night, this room glows like a light box. Luckily, the couple don't mind being stared at from the pavement – 'Sometimes we even play the jukebox and dance,' says John.

Carol moved to Norwich in 2008. 'After studying Textiles at Brighton, I lived in London and worked for a small studio, painting floral designs for textiles that sold to famous brands – Ted Baker, Nina Campbell, Lulu Guinness, Waverly, and some I am not allowed to name. I had a signature style, and recognition within the industry, but I was starting to want to do my own thing, under my own name, and in order to do that I needed to find a live/work space, and in order to be able to afford one, I knew I would have to look outside London.'

She settled on Norwich almost by chance. 'I happened to be invited to two parties here in the space of a year, and I did a bit of exploring. It is a beautiful city, and there are a lot of independent shops. It felt like somewhere I could settle, so I left Clapham, where I had lived for thirty years in three different houses, and

LEFT *At the end of the kitchen furthest from the shop, two antique chairs upholstered in Carol's floral fabric and a low coffee table make an informal seating area for morning coffee or afternoon tea on days when it is too cold or wet to sit outside.*

ABOVE *Much of Carol's work is to commission. This painting of a bouquet of garden flowers was for a bride, for whom it was digitally printed onto silk for her dress.*

OPPOSITE *Before John and Carol bought it, the property was being used as a café with serviced apartments above and a mess of shabby outbuildings at the back, including a catering shed and a disabled lavatory. All were demolished to make way for a single, large room, with three arched windows and arched French doors that open onto a lushly planted courtyard garden.*

OPPOSITE *Thanks to its surround of high wooden screening, the courtyard onto which the kitchen opens is private, and is also surprisingly quiet for a city centre. Paved in slate, it is furnished almost like a sitting room, with antique and vintage metal tables and chairs, and a wooden bench padded with flowery cushions. There is even a gilded and upholstered sofa, which is being left outside to 'weather', and over which the fast-growing creeper is already spreading its leaves.*

RIGHT *The kitchen is built against the old brick wall of the adjacent property, and the brickwork has been left bare above the wall covering of brick-shaped tiles. The oven sits in a tiled alcove and storage cupboards on either side have doors made from old French shutters.*

PAGES 180–181 *John describes Carol as someone who 'lives for flowers' and there are fresh flowers in every room, including flowers on fabrics, in paintings, on china, and on wallpaper, here dahlias from Norwich florist Jo Flowers. An antique glazed and painted cupboard holds kitchenware. To the left of it is Carol's desk and the area she uses as her studio, where she sits at a drawing board, to work on her paintings.*

found a place to rent just across the road from here, where I could use a room as a studio. Quite soon after arriving, I joined a small collective of artist-makers and moved into a flat above the shop next door. John was working as a consultant at the time, and was offering free mentoring for small businesses. When we met we made an immediate connection, and it was John who approached the owner of this place to ask if he would sell it to us.'

It is hard to imagine now, but at the time the shop was scruffy and being used as a café with cheap serviced apartments above. 'It wasn't hard to persuade him to let it go,' says John. 'The whole place was seedy and run-down.' With the help of an architect,

Carol designed a completely new extension at the back, separated from the shop by a glass partition with glazing bars that echo the proportions of the shelving in the shop – 'She's an absolute perfectionist when it comes to anything visual,' says John.

Three arched Crittall windows and a matching set of French doors were especially made to run along one side of this extension, again to Carol's specifications, and these open onto a courtyard garden, lush with creepers, jasmine, and pots of ferns, agapanthus, lavender, and hydrangeas. Furnished with two sets of tables and chairs, a bench, and a gilded sofa that is being left outside to 'weather', in summer it feels like a verdant outdoor drawing room.

RIGHT *The two rooms directly above the shop are accessed up a narrow staircase behind a discreet jib door in the back room of the shop. A pair of glazed double doors from the sitting room at the front open into a library and television room, where an array of Carol's bright cushions enliven the dark grey linen of the corner sofa. Walls are painted in two shades of green, and the floorboards are painted glossy black.*

OPPOSITE *The first-floor living room looks across the street to a row of Georgian houses opposite, in one of which Carol lived and worked when she first came to Norwich. The pair of sofas, covered in her own floral fabrics, are two of the few pieces of furniture she brought with her.*

From the back room of the shop Carol sells silk scarves, ties, and cashmere-lined stoles, wallpaper, shirts, and even shoes, all printed with her flower paintings. From here, a jib door in a side wall opens onto a steep staircase that first reaches a long, narrow room with a lavatory and a washbasin, and then, a few more steps up, the living room, where sofas are pulled up to a fireplace full of candles, and glazed double doors lead into a library at the back. Up another flight of stairs, there is a bedroom and bathroom resplendent with an antique metal bathtub and curvy washbasin from Stiffkey Bathrooms, who occupy the shop next door.

Uniting all these rooms, and the shop, is the recurring theme of flowers: flowers in vases; printed flowers in printed frames; flowers on upholstery and cushions; a trail of painted flowers looping across the bedroom wardrobes; books on flowers piled on the coffee table, and lined up on shelves. 'Carol lives for flowers,' says John. At one end of the kitchen is her drawing board, and a trolley houses her paints and an ice tray in which she mixes colours. An easel holds a finished work, a painted bouquet, commissioned by a bride and translated by Carol onto her wedding dress.

Much of Carol's work is bespoke. You can buy scarves, cushions, and shoes in the shop, and some clothing, but thanks to digital printing you can also commission a painting of favourite flowers, then have the design printed on anything from napkins to curtain fabric. Last year she was asked to design the interior of a new Turkish restaurant nearby, for which she came up with a scheme of flooring based on Iznik tiles, and murals blown up from a Victorian painting of women bathing in a hammam. 'It's the kind of thing that wouldn't have happened if I had stayed in London,' she says.

OPPOSITE *When Carol and John bought the shop, the rooms above it had been divided up to make serviced apartments. They have transformed these spaces to create a comfortable town apartment, here, on the top floor under the slope of the roof, a bedroom and bathroom (the lavatory is down the stairs on the same level as the living room). The bedroom end of this double room is painted white, but the floor throughout is the same gloss black as on the floor below.*

ABOVE *To the right of the bed, a small, gilded Italian chest of drawers stands below an alcove created by the old ceiling beams, the back wall of which has been painted dark grey as a foil to the bright green and white of leaves and flowers.*

ABOVE RIGHT *Carol and John collaborated with the owners of Stiffkey Bathrooms, the shop next door, when it came to the remodelling of the courtyard, the right-hand wall of which they share with the Stiffkey shop. They also bought from Stiffkey the curvaceous antique washbasin on its metal stand, and the French bateau bathtub.*

RIGHT *Carol painted the mosaic border on the floor around the bathtub, using two coats of Airfix enamel paint, and leaving a few squares missing for an authentic look of ancient Rome. The window is screened by a panel of antique lace suspended from a gilded French pelmet/valance. Here, as everywhere in the house, there are plants in pots, adding a splash of greenery to the retro glamour of the decor.*

SOURCES

ARCHITECTURAL SALVAGE

Lassco
Brunswick House
30 Wandsworth Road
London SW8 2LG
+ 44 (0)20 7394 2100
www.lassco.co.uk
A huge stock of everything from fireplaces to floors to stained glass, panelling, and staircases. Visit their website for details of their branches in Bermondsey and Oxfordshire.

Oak Beam UK
Ermin Farm
Cricklade Road
Cirencester
Gloucestershire GL7 5PN
+ 44 (0)1285 869 222
www.oakbeamuk.com
Reclaimed oak beams salvaged from Britain and France.
www.oldoakfloor.com
Antique oak floor boards from France.

Norfolk Reclaim Ltd
Helhoughton Road
Fakenham
Norfolk NR21 7DY
+ 44 (0) 1328 864743
www.norfolkreclaim.co.uk
Reclaimed building materials including bricks, pantiles and paving, plus architectural antiques and furnishings.

Retrouvius
1016 Harrow Road
London NW10 5NS
+44 (0)20 8960 6060
www.retrouvius.com
Fabulous stock of reclaimed and repurposed antique and vintage furnishings and fittings.

Wells Reclamation
Coxley
Wells
Somerset BA5 1RQ
+ 44 (0)1749 677087
www.wellsreclamation.com
Five and a half acres of architectural salvage, reclaimed building materials, antique and vintage furnishings.

BATHROOMS

Antique Bathrooms of Ivybridge
Erme Bridge Works
Ermington Road
Ivybridge
Devon PL21 9DE
+44 (0)1752 698250
www.antiquebaths.com
Reconditioned antique baths, plus reproduction ranges.

Balineum
www.balineum.co.uk
Online bathroom fittings and accessories, and a choice of pretty hand-painted tiles.

C P Hart
Newnham Terrace
Hercules Road
London SE1 7DR
+44 (0)20 79025250
and branches
www.cphart.co.uk
Inspiring bathroom showrooms.

Stiffkey Bathrooms
89 Upper St Giles Street
Norwich NR2 1AB
+44 (0)1603 627850
www.stiffkeybathrooms.com
Antique sanitaryware plus their own range of reproduction bathroom accessories.

The Water Monopoly
16-18 Lonsdale Road
London NW6 6RD
+44 (0)20 7624 2636
www.thewatermonopoly.com
Opulent period baths, basins, and fittings.

FABRICS

Bennison Fabrics
16 Holbein Place
London SW1W 8NL
+44 (0)20 7730 8076
www.bennisonfabrics.com
Chintzes, florals, stripes, and damasks.

Chelsea Textiles
13 Walton Street
London SW3 2HX
+44 (0)20 7584 5544
www.chelseatextiles.com
Embroidered cottons, delicate prints, linens, silks, and voiles with a distinctly 18th-century feel.

Colefax and Fowler
110 Fulham Road
London SW3 6HU
+44 (0)20 7244 7427
www.colefax.com
Quintessentially English fabrics and wallpapers, but also excellent for checks, ginghams, and stripes.

GP & J Baker
Unit 10 Ground Floor
Design Centre East
Chelsea Harbour
London SW10 0XF
+44 (0)20 7351 7760
www.gpjbaker.co.uk
Comprehensive range of fabrics including both traditional and contemporary.

Ian Mankin
269/271 Wandsworth Bridge Road
London SW6 2TX
+44 (0)20 7722 0997
www.ianmankin.co.uk
Natural fabrics, including unbleached linens, butter muslin, and striped tickings.

Lewis & Wood
105–106 First Floor
Design Centre East
Chelsea Harbour
London SW10 0XF
+44 (0)20 7751 4554
www.lewisandwood.co.uk
At the grander end of decorating with large-scale fabrics and wallpapers.

Russell & Chapple
30-31 Store Street
London WC1E 7QE
+44 (0)20 7836 7521
www.randc.net
Artist's canvas in various weights, jutes, fine muslin, deckchair canvas, and hessian sacking.

Susan Deliss
www.susandeliss.com
Gorgeous bespoke fabrics, including antique and exotic embroideries, cushions, and ikat lampshades.

Tinsmiths
8a High Street
Ledbury
Herefordshire HR8 1DS
+44 (0)1531 632083
www.tinsmiths.co.uk
Handwoven and printed textiles, including washed linens, African indigo cottons, and Indian block prints, plus lighting, studio ceramics, blankets, and cushions.

Thornback & Peel
www.thornbackandpeel.co.uk
Fresh screen-printed cottons, including their instantly recognizable 'Pigeon and Jelly', 'Pea Pod', and 'Rabbit and Cabbage' designs.

ANTIQUE FABRICS

Katharine Pole
+44 (0)774 761 6692
www.katharinepole.com
Wonderful selection of antique textiles, including toiles, plain linens, and stripes

Talent for Textiles
www.talentfortextiles.com
Contact Caroline Bushell on +44 (0)1404 45901 or Linda Clift on +44 (0)1305 264914.
Organizers of antique textiles fairs, bringing together dealers from all over the country in a series of attractive locations.

FITTINGS

Brass Foundry Castings
+44 (0)1424 845551
www.brasscastings.co.uk
More than 800 brass and foundry castings for furniture, doors and clocks reproduced from 17th- to 20th-century originals, available online or mail order only.

Clayton Munroe
+44 (0)1803 865700
www.claytonmunroe.com
Traditional handles, iron hinges, and latches, available mail order only.

FURNITURE – contemporary

The Conran Shop
81 Fulham Road
London SW3 6RD
+44 (0)207 589 7401
and branches
www.conranshop.co.uk
Tasteful modern furniture and accessories that mix well with antiques and look good in older buildings.

Heal's
196 Tottenham Court Road
London W1T 7LQ
+44 (0)20 7636 1666
and branches
www.heals.com
Good-quality contemporary furniture.

MADE
www.made.com
Online store selling a range of contemporary furniture sourced directly from the makers.

OKA
www.okadirect.com
Good-quality, mid-price furnishings in classic contemporary and traditional styles.

SCP
135-139 Curtain Road
London EC2A 3BX
+44 (0)20 7739 1869
www.scp.co.uk
Manufacturer and retailer of the work of contemporary British designers, including Matthew Hilton.

FURNITURE – antique, vintage and traditional

After Noah
261 King's Road
London SW3 5EL
+44 (0)207 3512610
www.afternoah.com
An appealing mix of antique, vintage, and contemporary furnishings, including cast-iron beds, lighting, and toys.

Alfies Antiques Market
13–25 Church Street
London NW8 8DT
+44 (0)20 7723 6066
www.alfiesantiques.com
Vintage, retro, and antique furnishings, and a good source of mid-century modern.

Bed Bazaar
The Old Station
Station Road
Framlingham
Suffolk IP13 9EE
+44 (0)1728 723756
www.bedbazaar.co.uk
Antique metal and wooden beds and handmade mattresses to order.

Crowman Antiques
54 Northgate Street
Devizes
Wiltshire SN10 1JJ
+44 (0)1380 725548
English country furniture, treen, and silver.

The French House
The Warehouse
North Lane
Huntington
York YO32 9SU
+44 (0)1904 400561
www.thefrenchhouse.co.uk
All manner of French antiques, from armoires to birdcages and baths.

George Smith
589 Kings Road
London SW6 2EH
+44 (0)20 7384 1004
www.georgesmith.com
Capacious and relaxed traditional sofas and armchairs.

Joanna Booth Antiques
+44 (0)20 7352 8998
www.joannabooth.co.uk
Early and rare antiques including sculpture and tapestries.

Max Rollitt
Yavington Barn
Lovington Lane
Avington
Hampshire SO21 1DA
+44 (0)1962 791124
www.maxrollitt.com
*(Showroom open by appointment)
Fine antiques as well as bespoke furniture design.*

Robert Young Antiques
68 Battersea Bridge Road
London SW11 3AG
+44 (0)20 7228 7847
www.robertyoungantiques.com
Fine English furniture and folk art.

Swaffer Antiques
30 High Street
Arundel
West Sussex BN18 9AB
+44 (0)1903 882132
www.spencerswaffer.com
Pretty shop with glamorous stock.

Talisman
79-91 New Kings Road
London SW6 4SQ
+44 (0)20 7731 4686
www.talismanlondon.com
Inspiring mix of unusual antiques.

FLOORING

Alternative Flooring Company
www.alternativeflooring.com
Coir, sea-grass, sisal, jute and wool floor coverings.

Bernard Dru Oak
www.oakfloor.co.uk
Specialists in the supply and installation of English oak flooring and parquet design, made from wood from the company's own woodlands.

Crucial Trading
www.crucial-trading.com
All types of natural floorings, most of which can also be ordered as rugs bound with cotton, linen, or leather.

Delabole Slate
www.delaboleslate.co.uk
Riven slate or slate slabs quarried in Cornwall and suitable for work surfaces, landscaping, fireplaces, and flooring.

Roger Oates Design
www.rogeroates.com
All kinds of natural floorings, including chunky abaca, plus flat-weave rugs and runners in chic stripes of gorgeous colour combinations.

Rush Matters
www.rushmatters.co.uk
Rush matting made with English rushes, also baskets and rush seating for chairs.

Solid Floor
61 Paddington Street
London W1U 4JD
+44 (0)20 7486 4838
www.solidfloor.co.uk
Quality wooden floors made from sustainable timber.

Woodworks by Ted Todd
London Design Centre
79 Margaret Street
London W1W 8TA
+44 (0)20 7495 6706
www.woodworksbytedtodd.com
Reclaimed, new, and antique timber flooring and joinery.

HEATING

Bisque
244 Belsize Road
London NW6 4BT
+44 (0)20 7328 2225
www.bisque.co.uk
Suppliers of classic fin radiators.

Jamb
95–97 Pimlico Road,
London SW1W 8PH
+ 44 (0)20 7730 2122
and at
8525 Melrose Avenue
West Hollywood
CA 90069
United States
+1 310 315 3028
Very high quality reproduction antique fireplaces, also antique fireplaces, reproduction lighting, and an extremely smart selection of antique furnishings

The Windy Smithy
+44 (0)7866 241783
www.windysmithy.co.uk
Bespoke woodburning stoves.

FINISHING TOUCHES

Charlene Mullen
7 Calvert Avenue
London E2 7JP
+44 (0)20 7739 6987
www.charlenemullen.com
Quirky homewares, including cushions, prints and ceramics.

Pentreath & Hall
17 Rugby Street
London WC1N 3QT
+44 (0)20 7430 2526
www.pentreath-hall.com
Irresistible homewares.

Ryder & Hope
30 Broad Street
Lyme Regis
Dorset DT7 3QE
+44 (0)1297 443304
www.ryderandhope.com
Stylish, contemporary artisan crafts.

KITCHENS

deVOL
36 St John's Square
London EC1V 4JJ
+44 (0)20 3879 7900
www.devolkitchens.co.uk
Handcrafted English kitchens.

Fired Earth
www.firedearth.com
Timeless kitchens and bathrooms; also an excellent range of paint colours.

Plain English
+44 (0)1449 774028
www.plainenglishdesign.co.uk
Elegant, simple wooden kitchens for traditional and period interiors.

PAINT

Edward Bulmer Natural Paint
+44 (0)1544 388 535
www.edwardbulmerpaint.co.uk
Eco-friendly paints in a wonderful selection of historic colours developed by architectural historian and interior designer Edward Bulmer.

Farrow & Ball
+44 (0)1202 876141
www.farrow-ball.com
Unbeatable for subtle paint colours with strange names, also papers, primers and limewash.

Francesca's Paints Ltd
+44 (0)20 7228 7694
www.francescaspaint.com
Traditional limewash, eco-emulsion paint, and chalky emulsion.

Paint and Paper Library
3 Elystan Street
London SW3 3NT
+44 (0)20 7823 7755
www.paintlibrary.co.uk
Excellent quality paint, including innumerable shades of off-white.

Papers and Paints by Patrick Baty
4 Park Walk
London SW10 OAD
+44 (0)20 7352 8626
www.papersandpaints.co.uk
In addition to their own excellent paints, this company will mix any colour to order.

LIGHTING

John Cullen
561–563 Kings Road
London SW6 2EB
+44 (0)20 7371 5400
www.johncullenlighting.co.uk
Extensive range of light fittings and a bespoke lighting design service.

Vaughan
+44 (0)20 7349 4600
www.vaughandesigns.com
Comprehensive range of replica period lighting from lamps to sconces to chandeliers.

WALLCOVERINGS

Cole & Son Ltd
+44 (0)20 7376 4628
www.cole-and-son.com
Wonderful wallpapers, from the traditional to the wacky.

De Gournay
112 Old Church Street
London SW3 6EP
+44 (0)20 7352 9988
www.degournay.com
Reproductions of hand-painted 18th-century Chinese wallpapers – the sort of thing you might use in a chateau.

PICTURE CREDITS

1 The home of Anita Evagora and David Campbell; **2** The home of Gavin Waddell; **3** The home of a stone carver in the Cotswolds; **4–5** The London home of Charlene Mullen; kitchen by Dive Architects; **6** The home of Gavin Waddell; **8–21** A Georgian terraced house in London, designed by Robert and Josyane Young of Rivière Interiors. www.robertyoungantiques.com; **22–35** The home of Anita Evagora and David Campbell; **36–49** The home of Jack Brister and Richard Nares in Frome, Somerset; **50–59** The Reilly home in Deal, Kent; **60–73** The home of Gavin Waddell; **74–87** The home of photographer Jan Baldwin; **98–109** The home of Frank Hollmeyer and Robert Weems; **110–123** A Charles II Period London Townhouse designed by Robert and Josyane Young of Rivière Interiors; **124–135** The home of Lucy Bathurst of Nest Design; **136–149** The home of a stone carver in the Cotswolds; **150–161** The London home of Charlene Mullen; kitchen by Dive Architects; **162–173** Melanie Molesworth, freelance interiors stylist. **174–185** The Norwich studio and home of Carol Lake, www.carollake.co.uk; **186** The Reilly home in Deal, Kent; **187** A Charles II Period London Townhouse designed by Robert and Josyane Young of Rivière Interiors: **188** The home of Jack Brister and Richard Nares in Frome, Somerset; **192** *left* The home of Lucy Bathurst of Nest Design; **192** *centre* The home of photographer Jan Baldwin; **192** *right* A Charles II Period London Townhouse designed by Robert and Josyane Young of Rivière Interiors.

BUSINESS CREDITS

Anita Evagora and David Campbell
Artworks by David Campbell
E: david@evagoracampbell.co.uk
Part of the house is available to rent as a holiday let.
www.atelier22york.com
E: info@atelier22york.com
Pages 1, 22–35.

Jack Laver Brister
Antiques dealer
Instagram: @tradchap
Pages 36–49, 188.

Carol Lake
www.carollake.co.uk
Pages 174–185.

Charlene Mullen
www.charlenemullen.com
see also
Dive Architects
www.divearchitects.com
Pages 4–5, 150–161.

Jan Baldwin
www.janbaldwin.co.uk
see also
Neisha Crosland
www.neishacrosland.com

and
Larusi Rugs
www.larusi.com
Pages 74–87, 192 centre.

Lucy Bathurst
www.nestdesign.co.uk
Pages 124–135, 192 left.

Melanie Molesworth
Molesworth & Bird
www.molesworthandbird.com
and
The Arched House
www.thearchedhouse.com
Pages 162–173.

Robert and Josyane Young
Rivière Interiors
(Rivière Interiors is incorporated in Robert Young Antiques.)
www.robertyoungantiques.com
Pages 8–21, 110–123, 187, 193 right.
Specialist decoration by
DKT ARTWORKS
www.dkt.co.uk
Pages 8–21.

INDEX

ACKNOWLEDGMENTS

A book is a team effort and I am lucky to work with a great team. Photographer Jan Baldwin is a joy – she takes wonderful photographs, and she makes me laugh. Her name and mine are on the cover of the book, but behind the scenes at Ryland Peters & Small are the people who make it all happen: Cindy Richards as Publisher; Julia Charles as Editorial Director; Leslie Harrington as Art Director; and Gordana Simakovic as Production Manager. The people I work most closely with are Jess Walton, who is a brilliant researcher, and Annabel Morgan, who is a brilliant editor, while Toni Kay juggles Jan's pictures and my words to make the pages look as good as possible. I couldn't ask for a finer group of colleagues and collaborators.

When it comes to finding locations, some of the best come by word of mouth. Many kind and helpful people made suggestions, but I would particularly like to thank Pablo Bronstein, Ursula Falconer, Roger Oates, and Dinah Hall. Also hugely helpful and encouraging were Mary Scott and Silvana de Soissons, aka The Foodie Bugle in Bath. As for the owners of the houses featured, they were, without exception, welcoming and generous.